£1
/15

POETRY NOW

HEADLINES IN VERSE

1993

Edited by Veronica Hannon

First published in Great Britain in 1993 by
POETRY NOW
1-2 Wainman Road, Woodston,
Peterborough, PE2 7BU

Foreword

I remember one lunch time sitting in my grandmother's sitting room just before the Sunday meal was served, watching the news. The headlines referred to a tragedy at Hillsborough football ground. Needless to say my curiosity was stimulated, as nothing attracts people's attention more than a disaster.

What I was unprepared for was the emotional impact that this event was to have on me. A picture flashed up of a football ground awash in a sea of flowers, within minutes I was in tears.

Operation Irma is another prime example of how the news can stir the emotions of people from many nations.

The writers in this anthology have been touched to the core by the stories presented in the news. They have been driven to put their emotions down on paper; desperate to make sense of the information they receive. This is the stuff that poetry is made of: the will to communicate. Their poetry is as vital and alive as the news in today's headlines.

One of the most difficult things about editing this collection was having to limit the book to two hundred poems. The poetry we received had such a depth of commitment and such important comments to make on the world in which we live, that it soon became obvious what an important and relevant book it would be both for today and for future generations.

Covering a wide range of styles, from free verse to tightly written rhyme, these poems speak with wit and insight and above all, honesty. Each one demands to be read and re-read. They offer the reader undeniable proof of the hope that poets can provide.

Contents

Battered Wife Who Killed Wins Freedom

Part I

In England, while reading the Guardian
I dust the memory of a moist kiss
And count stars
For every man I survived.

First, she tried to be a good wife
Promising to adhere to all his wishes:
Not to laugh or dye her hair black
Or to eat green chilli;
Then she stole her husband's torch.

His charred body now lies
With arms permanently raised against her.

Part II

In Chile, DINA, the secret police
Trained dogs to rape women.
Rats were also taught
To penetrate the same cavity.

Duty done, each day,
These same men returned home
To lie in a warm bed
Next to the better half of their humanity.

Clara Allen

Shards

Blame not the mechanical man of No. 10
or his slick side-kick next door.
Neither blame the wild blond man
stitched up by unforgiving friends.
They were all handed unclean shards.

Cast your mind back to 1979
when a coiffured, powder-blue clad lady
(hypocrisy is her middle name)
stood outside No. 10 intoning
Francis of Assisi's 'Prayer for Peace'.

The breaking of the unions
meant the destruction of the industrial base.
Napoleon was right: now Britain is a nation of shopkeepers.
The balance of payments is here to stay
because foreign goods are all we can buy.

Thatcherism promised the yuppies heaven
and while they gazed skywards
Lawson's yards and yards of plastic cards
opened a trapdoor to hell for the nation.
'Buy now, pay later with your shattered dreams!'

In 1988 the flatulent bubble of Thatcherism burst
leaving a terrible economic stench.
The miasma will not clear until
this Tory stable is cleansed.
That is, when the nation comes to its senses.

Homelessness, repossessions,
bankruptcies, suicides,
unending dole queues and ascending crime
are all there is to show
for a stubborn, ill-gotten gain.

Ivan Johnston

Killer Carried Human Hand as Trophy

Disasters are everyday as every
day becomes a disaster,
with distant dreams
of good old days
when there is no going back
because the killer carried human hand as trophy.

Everyone else is afraid to make a move
that'll leave them out of pocket,
so someone goes hungry
and eats the dove
and boils the bones for a stew
while the killer carried human hand as trophy.

There are bodies of evidence in shelled houses
that no-one can get close enough to cover,
so as it carries on
they go unburied
so all the world can watch
where the killer carried human hand as trophy.

And is this marking time 'til the end of time
as it spirals down in chaos?
Or just like normal
and another fine day
when it's in someone else's life
that the killer carried human hand as trophy.

Jason Cooke

Major Woos Faithful With Traditional Values

So, what's new . . . ?
Exemplified tautology,
glimpse of the obvious,
call it what you will.
Has it ever been known
for politicians to extol
*un*traditional values,
or throw back the shutters
to the fresh air of a new day,
shaking fusty bedlinen
of the taint of tradition
and malodorous decay?

On goes the hurdy-gurdy,
churning out its tinny tune,
without the antics of a monkey
to divert and maybe even
educate in some small way.
Let in the light . . . ?
No fear!
People might begin to question
a conditioning of generations;
worse still,
to think for themselves
and watch the sunbeams dance.

Rose Burnett

For Cyril

They are all dying:
The beautiful people.
Leaving us only
The ugly and the mediocre.
How earnestly we aspired
To hitch our ramshackle waggon
To the blazing trail
Of their shooting star.
To bask in the incandescent glory
Of their psychedelic parabola.
Better by far to dance
Amidst the constellations
Than gavotte, restrained and stately,
About the orbiting satellite
Sending out its signal
Through the bands of time and space,
Salutations
From the void
To the void.

Kathryn Hunt

Pensioners Live in Fear

Pensioners live in fear
It says here
The old bolt their doors
At four
In advance of last light
And struggle their
Heavy limbs and tired lungs
Up unforgiving stairs
To lie all night
Awake and watchful
Swollen knuckles curled
Around life savings under the pillow
Secure as Fort Knox
But the young bastard
Just breaks the window
Steals the cash from under the nose
Of the sleeping widow
Jemmies the sash
And away we go
Two nights on the bevy and a ride with a tart
Waking
The widow dies
Of a broken heart
The council says these flats offer
Relative safety
But relatives don't come near
They can't keep the lights on
Because of the cost
So the pensioners live in fear.

Fiona Ackroyd

6

Man Bites Dog

Confused
        and cornered
the genes somewhere
        do not interlock
biology accelerated
becomes demonic
leaving the faint whiff
of genocide,
In a wet nose
environment and destiny collide
        bollockless
strung up from a lamp post,
the musty smell of dog
        and the tang of cod liver oil

Chris Knighton

POW

(Ex-prisoner of war who slept in 'cage' died of pheumonia.
I.M. Kazimerz Symanski)

From our capital
he barricaded his door.
His flat was his cell.

The kitchen lino
is patterned with excrement.
Gunge claws up the sink.

The utilities
are long disconnected; yet
still he feared the gas.

His cooker is old
and terribly corroded.
His bed is a cage

for security.
The tortured enough body
has sniffed an escape.

Tim Youngs

Monkey World

Chimpanzee clan in the wild,
Mother chimpanzee with child.

Other chimpanzees defend,
Eight adults murdered in the end.

Spanish beach photographer
Pulls her teeth with household pliers,

Burns her face with cigarette,
Drugs, beats, worse to stop her bite.

Then Pedro works beside the sea:
'You hold cuddly chimpanzee?'

Snap! Good money and a tan.
Man-like ape and ape-like man.

Madonna and adopted child.
Dead at eight, 'til forty wild.

Duncan Forbes

Planet Celluloid

It flickered in the night,
Unnamed I had to find,
What kind of life it held,
In Sector number nine.

Let's cruise to planet Celluloid,
A skull shaped planet asteroid,
Projected on the screen of night,
Like its stars in black and white.

Shape shifters of the highest form
True humans they'd never seen
Only from the waves they'd picked up
From our TV screens.

To make us feel at home, they'd changed their planet's surface,
From barren land to movie set, one to suit their purpose.

Planned this meeting long, a great but dying race,
Changed from Insect Alien form, picked a brand new face.

Their leader took a form,
That was pleasing to his eye,
and there to greet us when we landed
Karloffs Frankenstein

With open arms they're greeting us,
Wanted us to stay,
With *our* arms we are just like Mankind,
Blew them all away.

Let's cruise from planet Celluloid,
That skull shaped planet asteroid,
Spinning silent on the night,
Not a creature left in sight.

Mark Mawston

Repentant

Never was a day so strange
So fierce, intense, yet cheated
As the day I saw
A baby - its heart born outside
Its body
As if to say
'This is how I want to live!
To show myself from the very start
Uncovered, open, alive
To the world's touch'
But they safely hid its heart
Before it beat but a few
Free hours - unabashed.
Shouting its challenge to the world
'This is how to live!'
They put it away and
There it stays - beating in time
To a cowed tune
More thoughtful now
Repentant.

Miles Craven

Les Dawson Dies at Fifty Nine

A short, rotund man in an electric blue suit
Stands centre stage under a listless spotlight.
He sweats. He breathes heavily.
He is in a room chill with cruelty.
The audience stare at him
As enemy has faced enemy since Cain faced Abel.
They are ignoring every word.
He has told them every joke,
Sung them every song,
Recited every comic verse.
He is ready to walk off to his 'dressing-room'
With the broken mirror and three-legged chair
'Provided by the management'.
But he takes a deep breath
And wipes away the salty rivulets above his top lip.
He speaks again. But this time with more resonance . . .
With more stature . . . With more anger.
'You've made me feel as welcome here as my mother-in-
law at my house. I always know when she's coming to visit.
The mice start throwing themselves on the traps!'
Silence. Then a single, female laugh. Followed by two . . .
Make that five more! They are chased around the room by
two hundred more!
His breathing relaxes. His fingernails no longer cut
into the palms of his hands. A star is born!
And now, unbelievably, he has died.

Alan Wightman

12

My Husband Has Breasts

My husband has developed breasts.
I am writing to you in the hope
That you can help other people in a similar position
By printing this in your magazine
(Which I know is sold up and down the country
To women who want to learn
How to live life to the full).

My husband has developed breasts.
We just woke up one morning
And there they were,
Like two perfect peaches

Pert and perfect peaches.

It was such a shock that
Neither of us could face our breakfast,
Let alone the neighbours.

Everywhere we turn
Breasts haunt us.

I have completely gone off sex.

My husband has developed breasts and I'm
At my wits end.

Please help.

Worried, Thetford.

Angie Pell

13

Fury as Judge Calls Raped Girl, Eight, No Angel

There was a little girl
who had a little curl
and a taste for doctors and nurses.
To be any good
she had to be very, very good
But since she was not,
she was
      worthless.

Jill Dawson

Stand the IRA up Against a Wall and Shoot Them!

That would solve everything, wouldn't it?
Taking one extreme to another,
Kill one victim to avenge the other;
Is that the most intelligent solution you have to offer?

Do we really have this thirst for blood?
An eye for an eye and the triumph of good.
So the media can sit in judgement
As we give them our support,
Absorbing every word
Each sensation-seeking, attention-hungry, opinion-creating
Journalist might report.

Karen Hilditch

A Mountain's Shame

At twenty six thousand feet, on the South Col
lies the debris of expeditions:
yellow cylinder upon yellow cylinder
unharvested pumpkins
preserved for ever
in the rare air.

Beside them, other discarded
relics
human relics
Sherpas who have carried air
on their backs
have carried life
lie here, shrouded in tenting
unclaimed.

Cylinders can be gathered in
but a Sherpa's spirit will wander
without rest
until taken from this bleak
open grave
and released
on the funeral fire.

Jo Phillips

Suicide

*(A Staffordshire teacher who was sacked for locking a suicide risk
pupil in a room has lost his claim for unfair dismissal)*

Your mind is bathed in guilt and pain
over the cruel affair
locked an innocent in a room
and then -

You left him there.

Is there any pleasure by
hurting a young child
I think not, so face the consequences.

So now you face the wrath of God
on your Judgement Day
and people stay to witness fun
as your soul is stole away.

Could you be forgiven
No, I think you cannot
so we'll see how you feel in your own

Captivity.

Scott Munro (16)

17

Film Scheme for the Blind

(The Chapter Arts Centre in Cardiff is to employ a describer . . . for film screenings to act as eyes for the blind - partially sighted)

The lights dim.
They had been bright for some,
Bright with the promise of a silver screen,
Filled with colour, wide-screen wonder, images of romance.

For others, bright and dim are equal.
Not even black and white, just grey.

But they have their own light, a voice
Murmuring in head-phoned ears.

And what a voice:
Seductive, silken, strident, sibilant,
Weaving a chromic pattern of sound.
Telling a tale to fascinate,
To draw tears, to win smiles,
To make the heart rise up
And the mind sigh with pleasure.
To mount to a climax and end with a dying fall.

Lights up - and how they clap the head-phoned ones,
Faces alight with joy
For them a film to end all films.

Odd, then, that those who saw that film
Sit with hands in laps,
Unmoved by what they saw,

Feeling, in some way
Deprived.

Christopher Haines

Rapists and Arsonists Stay in Cosy Bedrooms

Rapists and arsonists stay in cosy bedrooms
with an eye on the future, like sparks, or drowning landmines;
Vipers in the heart of smalltowns, sitting squat as machines,
chuffing out waste and smoke and itching for the road,
to explode, into needles of fiery desire.

Rapists and arsonists stay in cosy bedrooms and
travel deep into the black heart's bile,
while slashed movies roll round their Tube-map heads;
Whole plum-dark confessions slide as on a screen, before their
videotape eyes, silent violence, eyes unsmiling orbits,
dim suns fading the age.
Inside they bleed, like women, or shot cops.

She walks past and looks toward the lamplit chamber, as a sunflower
stretches before the glow in its perennial search for the source of
light.
The gingham bustle and the murderous exchange of gazes: in an
hour the pedestrians chase,
In two she'll be dead, her head bent West to Mecca.
God *does* play dice with the universe and what's worse he does it
with a poker face, and so she lies there as he has lived -
inert and hurt and often horizontal.

Back in his womb-room he sits, still as a painted life,
wiping blood from the long greedy knife. Smeared linen
struggles on the washing line outside, whilst inside the fire is
        doused, quiescent for now, the fuck rubbed off.
Curtains close and the head lies to rest and the
birds leave the wires, in a million directions, hard and fast
        and loose as words.

Jim Pollock

Norman's Knife

Sinking ships can't be saved from sinking,
Backbenchers cannot be stopped from thinking
that it's government by opinion poll.
That was the crash, so what's my role?
Thirty six hour politics!
Policy as conjuring tricks!
A sugar-coated rate cut for a Daily Mail cover,
As they wince at the pain we make with another.
I conclude this was a Major mess, right from the start.
So I put a knife in his back. He hasn't got a heart.

The smile is important. I must keep smiling,
Even as I gain another shoulder blade.
How could you do this to me Norman?
You were my human shield.
But what is there for me now?
Consciences that yawn loudly as they wake.
Skeletons that rattle in their cupboards.
Stalking-horses that neigh in the shadows.
Who can be trusted?
A Clarke, A Portillo - even a Bottomley,
Could finish me off, and steal the crown. Oh Yes!
Torn by The Times and burnt by The Sun.
Take me back to dear old Brixton!

Kev McCready

Camillagate

Picked out of the ether
By a snooping antenna
Lovey-dovey chitchat between Charles and Camilla
Intimate slush
About towels and such
Are taped and transcribed for The Mirror.

Thomas Slemen

Young Failing to Seek Early AIDs Treatment

Infection apprehends the life
From destiny's untroubled calm,
Unable to incise the knife
The angels watch disease embalm;
Preserved from early banishment
Towards uncertain afterlife
Yet locked within an open tent
This prison holds the stillborn life:
Should angels never wield the blade,
With life lives love - don't be afraid.

John Michael Bennett

Landslip Brings Hotel to Cliff Edge

The metaphors fell heavily
Like English summer rain
A hotel sliding down a cliff,
the country's down the drain.
But who's to say that
Scarborough's loss
might not be Brighton's gain.

Yorkshire may be slipping
and the government in hock
But the B and B's of Blackpool
are built on solid rock.
The landladies of Scarborough
will be toasting Britain's health
as they thank the underwriters
who signed away their wealth.

Gillian Williams

Docklands Pub

The bar is dim with evening light,
starlings settle on the trees like dust,
pigeons call against the coming night;
the park gates close, the dock gates rust.

These men are playing cards, intent
upon each ace or joker in the pack;
their hands are soft with rest - they lent
them once to work, which dealt them back.

They're drinking playschool beer -
just halves - they can't afford the bliss
of getting paralytic drunk in here:
just this pretence of being on the piss.

The last ship's being plated in the yard,
the dole will trump each welder, fitter -
one bottle swung into the prow, smashed hard:
enough champagne to sour their bitter.

They watch the news and laugh at interest rates,
their empty slipways haunt the estuary,
they cut the pack and deal it to their mates,
the future's hull is holed far out to sea.

They're streetwise and, though life is shit,
they're laughing, gambling, doing deals,
if they could gaze Fate in the eye they'd spit:
'Play on, you know the fucking rules!'

Graham Mort

Violence Erupts on Germany's Day of Atonement

I forgot that I was of gypsies
and nothing should touch us:
misled myself into your space,
with no wrap but the wall.
By the hearth spun an earring's light,
making the papers;
while my guileless tired face
nodded step to the ball.

On the ceiling your dancers crept,
shading a memory
of a past in their steppin' life
- Burn City Hall!
In the arms of you there I wept,
tasting inertia;
like a backwoods hick royal wife
tearing her shawl.

Mark Spry

Visitors Flock to See Vision of the Cross

'Hurry now William.'
She guides his feet to the floor
And obediently he stands.
Face lined and tired,
He hobbles, leaning on her
From bed to kitchen.
She leaves him seated at the cold stone sink,
Soap in hand, striped towel nearby,
And darts businesslike back.
She's been up for hours.
She throws open the flimsy window.
The spring light and bird song fill the room.
She dusts the small thirties table,
Moves the crucifix to centre stage.
Already the faithful are calling.
She unties her apron strings
Ready to greet the pilgrims to her grotto.
William calls.
He must wait.
'I have a house to run here but I'm getting very little done.'
She opens the door to the faithful.
In rush the white doves with dawn.
They flutter past Elizabeth and land
Around the gilded icons in her room.
She watches at the open door.
The rugged mountains overpower the scene
And still he calls.

Sue Thornton

The Reign of Taylor the Irrelevant

As apt today as all days, every day being much the same,
What began as a trivial pursuit
Has now gone far beyond a fatuous game.

A nation has quietly succumbed
To a most consumptive dependency.
The perpetually self-driven need
To gorge itself on it's own mediocrity.

First the delightfully bland taste of the word 'reign'
Now our monarchy has failed in a way predictably mundane.
To be Britain as our skies are to low pressures
'Reign, reign, go away, come again on Christmas Day'.

This headline makes our juices rise, or venom I should say.
But I'm not sure if it's the words themselves
As black and white always read grey nowadays.

But the true thrill is the England manager's name
(Was there not a prune stone once named after him?)
To one and all a cause célèbre
As he is the *sole* reason why England cannot win.

And the crime to provoke such armchair enmity?
Perhaps the attempt to inspire pride
In a country where the pride of the people
Has so long been viewed an irrelevance, it has died.

On whose hands does the blood of the red, white and blue lie?
Those who said 'society' is all in the mind?
Those pointing the way but never able to say
'I'm sorry, the fault is mine'

But a warning to all in positions of leadership,
If Taylor's blood whets our appetite
The love of still, grey waters might prove not to run so deep.
Sleep tight, Britain's leaders, sleep tight.

Anthony Chasteauneuf

Tories Lurch to Twelve Year Low

The latest polls catch one's eye
Major unpopularity, the paper's cry
Upheaval at Westminster
As our Prime Minister
Faces the consequence
Of Thatcherist opulence
And in his party's defence
He quotes lower inflation
'Bottom line interest rates'
For a paying nation
But what of the debt
Built up in boom years
When 'I'm all right Jack'
Was meeting our ears
The champagne stopped flowing
Unemployment rose
'Lucky to have a job'
Is how the nineties saying goes
Those years of affluence
Are taking their toll
The public lacks confidence
Says this latest poll.

Sara Louise Mudie

I Have Seen the Future and it Goes Topocketa Pocketa Pocketa

A hotel slides into the ocean
Countries fall apart
The world will shortly boil dry and
Crack
My transplanted heart
Corruption riddles the system
Bang
Splinters the ceiling of glass
The woman priest may well ask God
What
Has come to pass?
I have seen the future
Topocketa pocketa pock-
And those who came to praise it have probably
Stayed to mock
The eyes of the starving accuse us
The eyes of the dying
Dim
The homeless and mad harass us
Public transport's grim
To the rich the golden handcuffs
For the mugger the sand in the sock
For the rest of us the future
Goes topocketa pocketa pock -

M Windram Wheeler

Les Dies Laughing

Dawson the morose
archetypal English clown
earn a laugh from anything
that's supposed to get you down.
seaside camps,
landladies,
mum-in-law of course.
Filthy weather,
surgeries,
dilatory horse.
Les the laughing grumbler
scourge of bad news day.
Every dark cloud has a lining
(black, of course, he'd say).
seaside rooms,
mum-in-law,
married couple's row
women's troubles,
landladies,
nowhere near
so funny now.

Ray Bryant

Ode to England

England land of my heart's desire,
Country lanes, Earl Grey tea,
Sycophantic royal family.

Bluebells, roses, buttercups,
Party political flowers,
Tory heartland, England mainland,
Greater England towers.

Revolution, devolution,
The Welsh, the Scots the 'north',
Little England, which way now?
God knows nothing rhymes with north.

'Don't let Europe rule Britannia'
Protect us from insanity,
Euromadness, Deloresque culture,
Long live national sovereignty.

England land of my heart's desire,
Nostalgic opium for the ranks,
Nationalistic fervour, self importance,
European domination, no thanks.

Claire Boobbyer

Food for Thought

Of one hundred and nine reported rapes
There were only eight convictions
One hundred and nine
Eight
It doesn't add up

Now I'm a wizard with numbers
I eat numbers for breakfast
idly toying and playing with them before
striking
and digesting
But this I cannot swallow
These numbers simply don't
won't
Add up
I roll the statistics around
Try to soften them up a bit
But there they sit
set
They defy all attempted mastications

I spit them out
They are too bitter for my taste
They don't agree with me
and leave
a
nasty
sickening
feeling in my stomach

Catherine Woodall

33

The Harp

Under the burning crumble of the peat
Last spring, they found the harp.
A thousand years and more it lay
Unsung, the chords taut in buried hands
Of Celtic bards. The music curled asleep
Its strings still resin, taut - left full of woods
And sea and birds - like paintings in the earth
And only curlews mourning in a bleary sky above.

They lifted out the harp, a dozen heads
All bent and captured, listening for the sounds
That might lie mute inside - the bones of hands
That once had curled for kings. But all around
Were broken promises, the wreckage of the Viking lash
Across their history's face. The harp still played -
Remembered how to weep.

Kenneth C Steven

Going Down

Streets on fire with tar
The roads melted and asphalt was turned
Into streams of superheated
Gliding metal over which
You have no real control.

A lot of people have just come to look
For God's sake get help
There was a blinding flash
We can see people who are still alive
I saw a girl engulfed in flames from head to foot
A fireman could not bring himself to help her
The night just lit up.

Watching a top-rated soccer programme
Most residents stay behind locked doors at night
The other sickening species who feed on mayhem came out
A priest worked among the rescuers
The air was thick with the smell of perfume
Swathes of nearby trees burst into flame
Even police cars were not immune.

Two 747's full of passengers
Might collide over the West End
And go straight down on Soho
As the theatres are emptying.
Air thick with the smell of perfume
Oh God, we're going down.

James B L Hollands

A Centurion's Lament

I said unto one 'Go' and he goeth.
I said unto another 'Come' and he cometh.
They said unto me . . .

'Finito Benito'.

Good night, Vienna
The fat lady has started to sing.

To bring home the bacon -
A time honoured station, but
The train has come to a halt.
Though not totally gravy it was at least savoury -
There must be a fault on the line.
Written out of the script, a hero eclipsed,
A star given to fall and decline.

Or, maybe life begins at UB40?
Goodbye to motorway madness.
Farewell to British Rail cruelty.
Swap my sandwich for a sand-wedge,
Tend the garden, beg no pardon,
Ransomed Old King Cole.
'Would the next contestant sign on, please
Here's some money for passing stop'.
A consolation for being a flop.

'To our requirements, you are now surplus,
You no longer meet our purpose.
Your password has expired.
You are about to be retired.
So, there's a good chap, it's just a mishap.
Log off,
Bog off,
Be gone.'

Nick Wilde

Heart on the Line

The 'phone rings with a heart on the line,
I must stop crying for there is no time
To wait to answer that heart on the line.

No names, a voice from the unknown
Needs help so bad they have to 'phone
A stranger; a little voice all alone.

'Please help me, I don't know what to do
That's why I've left home to 'phone you.
You see, my daddy's a monster, but he's lovely too.'

After some time I put down the 'phone,
I was thinking of a girl all alone
With a version of love in her own home.

Love is what they say it is, somehow
Excuses and lies used to fetter
A young child's mind, not now, but forever.

Jerry Stephens

Everyday Images

Motionless,
black-skinned
and with protruding joints,
contorted where they lie,
they could be dead,
a thousand years preserved,
and dug from northern peat
except that, now and again,
they breathe.

And the incessant flies,
-concentrated on the nostrils,
mouths and eyes-
with the whitewashed walls
and shimmering haze, the dry-brown
dust-filled vista, tell us
this is another place,
and now,
and far away.

Terry Sweetman

Faro '92

June, the longest day. On shimmering air
White styrene plane banks lazily and turns,
Holds an instant against the azure blue
Then stalling, gracefully dips towards the
Cyan sea. Tremulous airy balance:
Carries and carries inches above sand.
A zephyr's kiss: wings tilt than dip and touch.
The cheap toy cartwheels, the child screams with joy.

Dark, deep, December. Fighting squalls of rain
Cumbrous DC 10 bucks the scudding winds,
Holds an instant against a livid sky.
Juddering down, down towards landing lights:
Trembling, carries beyond the boiling sea.
Katabatic gust: wings tilt, dip then touch.
Their world explodes apart, adults scream and cry.

Patrick B Osada

No Crime

I am case no. 65321DS
You are prisoner no. 74212ER
Am I the victim or the accused?
My ordeal is 'alleged'
You have committed 'no-crime'.
My suffering has absolved you of sin
You, Barrabas, are set free;
I am stripped, humiliated, crucified
The split-crack of my wounds
Refused - 'too disturbing for the jury',
My body segmented, dissected for perusal
My life examined, morality questioned.
You have committed 'no-crime'.
Murmurs, excuses of sympathy are stuffed in my ears
Like the fist rammed in my mouth to silence me,
They burn like the acid sear of a vinegar-soaked sponge
Growing, choking, mute in my throat.
Contrition - 'Broken in spirit by sense of sin'
But what is my sin?
'Corroboration insufficient, complainant unreliable'
Here is my sin: my body, my sex
Open for all to see;
Cracked, imperfect.
Now will they believe me?
But you have committed 'no-crime'.

Mary Wallace

The Women Child Abusers

The silence of trust makes their past pain sublime
Through the shield of awarelessness;
Love as a crime.

The adults of evils long disbelieved
Poison fresh cultures, exactly aggrieved.
It's a pasture of mutual bonded despair.
New children suffer like the grown ups who dare.
Years of hurt crawl into speechless heredity;
Extremities of feeling are bared by proximity.
Damaged while cradled, as they were before;
Inexplicably nervous, scared, scarred and sore.

The cycle of nature rots through its pain
Which, lifelong ignored, coyly happens again.
The hurt in the monster's heart, blindly maligned,
Is the trauma incarnate, the symptom in kind.
In kind adult caring, the tragedy lies
In a too-clinging legacy of fond-fondled ties.

The women of child abusers
You blissfully condemn
Do unto others merely what
Others have done to them.

Angela Kaye

Just Twenty Four Hours to Save Baby

Only ten months old,
and so small.
Just came into the world,
this baby girl.

Her beaming smile radiates from the page
like the sun, brightening my day.
But storm clouds gather above her soul.
As death waits to swipe her from her home.
The body is dying and so is she.
Two loving parents make a desperate plea,
'Help our daughter, save her please.
She needs a donor if she's to live.'
Just twenty four hours to save baby.
'Won't someone help . . . please?'

As the hours pass,
moments last,
Minds of the living,
keep hoping.

A beeping life support registers the breath,
of life living on the edge of death.
Her parents clutch the hands of the one they created,
only to see and feel their girl's life fading.
Black carpets the sky as far as the eye can see.
Whilst loving parents make a final plea,
'Help our daughter, save her please.
She needs a donor if she's to live.'
Just twenty four hours to save baby.
'Won't someone help . . . please?'

Soman Balan

Scenes From an Everyday War

Our cannibal diet is supplemented
by a vicious thieving for the eye;
the crisp flesh of newsprint
crackling with atrocious faces,
uncomfortably separated from our comfort
yet almost touching.
Does the sweat show in the camera-flash?
Does the shutter-speed crack open
the liquorice roots of teeth,
and make porcelain eggs of open eyes?
One day soon will there be blank pages?
Will the freak-show have departed,
leaving only
the caterpillar fingers of scholars
inching among archives?

David Haden

Untitled

Man bites dog
Phew, what a scorcher!
Athens police chief
guilty of torture

DJ in sex romp
Cliff death was murder
Rejected Maggie
goes into purdah

Porn free for kiddies
Soap star arrested
Bust pension fund
was 'under-invested'

Yuppie flu conquered
Store 'won't let pram in'
Five deaths an hour
in Sudanese famine

My 50-inch whoppers
World Cup disaster
British 'shirkers' must
learn to work faster

There's a Nip in the air
Chink of hope in Peking
US Marines capture
Commie black king

Death row sex date
Di gets an ovation
KGB suspects died
of defenestration

Keep taking the tabloids
(and the qualities too)
With news you can use
they are vital to you

Ken Creffield

Nature Confounds the Prophets of Doom

The tanker Braer smashed on rocks at Fitful Head,
And slimy, sluggish waves of crude oil spread,
Outwards like a virulent disease,
Where seals basked on sun warm rocks
In the clean blue seas.
Arctic Terns, shags and cormorants,
Whales, dolphins and porpoise in terror fled,
Unwilling victims of man's greed,
But nature became angry.
Storms tossed the oil away.
Surely as she covers old rail tracks with weeds,
And crashes cliffs into the seas
She flexed her muscles proving power.
Ice ages come and go and melt in pools,
The planets spin through space,
And puny man still thinks he rules.
Nature confounded the prophets of doom,
But she is still waiting there,
Watching our ignorant, weak endeavours,
To destroy her beauty and might
She is waiting for that final revenge,
When the prophets of doom will be proved right.

M Denwood

Jobless Down Again

I remember how the fire used to burn down low
and amber flickers settle to a crimson gleam,
                    lost among the coals,
and then soon there'd come the time when a bustling try,
quickly, at rescue was needed for it to revive,
                    not turn cool and fade,
a solemn fuss with newspaper and sticks, much blowing,
huffing, and a suspenseful pause for the wanted blaze.

Now an open hearth seems so much of the distant past,
and though I'm sure it's wrong to think that we were somehow
                    happier than today,
it seems at times that there are more of those among us
deaf to a call for a heartier kind of justice -
for it's quite OK just as long as it isn't us,
                    worth it for the price -
   and the frail but not unconvincing prop
   - its impressiveness of numbers, consensus -
   of an official statistical optimism
can lead to endless overlookings of omissions,
from a missed-out word to closed-out them - though the spread
                                        broadsheet
                    drawing up the draught,
encourages those flames that it conceals.

For the soul of communities may be like a furnace,
and never to let the fire within us burn down low,
                    never can be news;
yet I wonder what's mislaid of ambitions, dreams, goals,
(as the shifting of the cooled cinders, shrinking to fall),
                    lost within the figures,
                    down among the jobless.

Mike Booth

47

Lobsters Come Out of Their Shell

The Lobster comes out of his shell in the night
In the deep of the dark ocean tides
Creeps from his carapace, ghostly and bright
Revealing the spell of a lobster's insides

For none can describe him - this lobster, transformed
Dancing and floating through sea-paths of weed
The corals applaud, and fishes have swarmed
To set him alight on his curled sea-steed

Spiralled and shining, this gallant appears
Trailing long samphires and streamers of light
For the fire of a lobsterish knight, as he nears
His purpose, sends lesser shrimps fleeing with fright

Down through the wrecks and the wracks of the reef
He tumbles, to meet with his brothers arrayed
Alike in fire-colours, proclaiming belief
In the right and the might of the *Lobster Parade*!

Processional banners of cowrie and kelp!
The rainbowing dance, as the marchers fluoresce!
The meeting and mingling, with more come to help -
O magical sight, as the troops coalesce!

The triumph of lobsterdom rises and peaks!
But then - as in dream - a manta-ray sweeps
Nearby; in a flicker, the seabed is dark -
Dark is the ocean - and deep are the tides.

The lobster returns to his shell, in the night
Shrugs on his carapace, cosy and tight
To drift with the current and sing in the waves
Of shedding one's shell, in the secret sea-caves.

C S Thomas

Postcard From LA

Reached the city of angels,
Seemed much more like hell,
Fires were burning, the tide was turning
As far as I could tell.

Reached the city limit,
Left the rest behind,
Had to drive the freeway
For a united state of mind.

Did you get my letter,
D'ya get my postcard from LA,
Did you get my letter,
D'ya hear what I had to say.

Drove up to the mountains,
As far as I could go,
Cut myself off from the world
And everyone I know.

Gazed amazed in silence,
At the beauty that I found,
Then back to civilisation
And madness all around.

Met a psycho in San Francisco,
Didn't know if it was day or night,
Pacing the room up and down,
Said that he wanted to fight.

Martina on the plane to Heathrow,
Travelling through the night,
Helped me learn to laugh again
As we talked 'til morning light.

Dave Johnson

Strange Journey

An aged despot flicks his horsehair switch
But fails to turn the tide of democracy.
A latter-day Canute who cannot halt
The sea-change in his land-locked country.
He broke the chains of colonialism
Only to manacle Malawi
To a one party rule.
Prescribing agriculture for most,
Education for some.
Courting the architects of apartheid
And oppression,
A new capital was built on suspicion.
And silent bones.
Lilongwe.

In Kasungu the Kachere tree stands: proud
Monument to the early learning of the Ngwazi.
For Kamuzu is an educated man.
One doctor, whose cure has lost currency,
Completes a circuitous route
From the revered Kachere
Through the Liverpool poor to prison.
(For fighting against federalism)
In the lake-land of his birth.
Released, a hero of Independence.
Respected doctor. Benign dictator.
An aged despot sadly flicks his horsehair switch.

Tricia Morris

50

Scotland - Shut Down

(We beat the Kaiser and Hitler . . . now it looks like we're sunk by Riftund and Major)

They shut down railways, stopped the flow
To remote parts, a bitter blow.
Steel lines run silent, quiet, still,
Across Scottish moor and glen and hill.

They shut down shipyards on the Clyde,
Majestic ships once born with pride.
The towering cranes lie idle now,
Point dead men's fingers to the sky.

The assembly lines that moved so fast,
Where cars emerged, to run, to last.
Sleek product of Linwood's skilful men,
They shut you down, ne'er rise again.

They shut down pits, abandoned, dead,
Where miners strove and worked to live.
Where bounteous treasures still remain,
Their life's blood cut, was your revenge.

Rosyth, the Navy's Royal Base,
Warships sailed forth to save our race.
Withstood the o'erwhelming German might,
But now *you've* got her in *your* sights.

We watch their death throes, hear their scream
Why do *you* rob us of our dream?
No Trident refit, skills to sell,
Instead *you* offer a Nuclear hell.

Honour is dead where Tory dogma lives,
The English vote, to save you, holds the sway.
And promises given are haughtily brushed aside,
What do *you* care for Scottish workers' pride?

We are not humbled, nor yet cowed,
To Tory dogma we shall never kneel.
Bring forth your hidden courage and your pride,
This land of ours shall surely yet be free.

Margaret A R Czudek

Untitled

I see the hostages McCarthy and Keenan back
and I walk into the desert without a map.
My place in history booked
no one around, no one looked
as I put one foot into no man's land
me and the foolish German.
My Government will bargain for me
and we'll see news men hound from the spot
of where I just turned my back
to have a look at nothingness
desert, desolate
while at home my Government waits for the
green shoots
of recovery to barter more prominently
with
sit in jail, waiting for an offer from
The Sun.
Burn the midnight oil at noontime
time goes so slow here.
Bare essentials, enough to keep a
diary
for a weary world
told, of a fool out for glory
story's old
It's already been told
boldly go nowhere near no fly zones
where Iraqi jets marks the spot
blotting landscapes with British made jets
rest, not here. Because the dark is not
far away . . .

Karol Jones

Outside Interference Deemed a Nuisance

If delirium be my wont
And I find my drunken Parisienne caverns
And fear and love and ineptitude be my wont
And I find solace in candlelit damp,
then now is my birth hour
An injection of sugar.
And if outcast willows cannot shed light,
on these insular things that prey on the lonely,
Should the almighty it, not thunder and scorch its mark,
Impress me,
If these desires be unrequited,
Then come the hour not soon enough,
Time will find me.

Shane Whelehan

Silos to Rent Suitable for Growing Mushrooms

After they took the grave goods from the tomb
it was like this; after they lifted from the Hunn
princess's breast the skeleton of the spread eagle
and cleared the gold plaques from her bones
one by one; after they moved her to the museum
so they might sift her left bed of black earth
for lost finger rings and verdigrised ear bobs:

an absence, a great 'not' of unfilled socket,
the gape of a toothless mouth, a rifled nest,
discarded wrappings - anything purpose-built
whose motive has been snatched away and shed
like deciduous leaves when November comes . . .
the cold time of year, the Cold War god whose box
this was and from whence he was meant to spring

in winter, furling like dry ice from the opening
in the ground, hugging the ground, its contours,
riding its lifts and falls and long levels that
might as well be water to a conflagration -
the god broken and made again a thousandfold,
risen and rising athwart the sky, ascended as
dust and vapour over a level-as-water earth . . .

Cruise gone, the god gone, worship departed with the
symptoms of winter, the personage of the monument
long trundled away - only the little organisms move
behind the steel doors thick as a double bed's width,
only the mushrooms rising in the dark a thousandfold
and more from their shelves of black earth:
smell of mould, pale underground plaques as grave goods.

Annemarie Austin

Shame of our Head Teachers

Don't want to go to history,
Think I'll go and hide.
Who cares what happened in 1066,
Or when James 2nd died?

James and Suzy I just can't stand.
When they see me they always laugh.
'spose it's coz I wear glasses,
And they think they're really naff.

The headmaster hates me - can't think why
I don't give him cause for grief,
And though I talk in lessons
I always keep it brief.

Maybe that's the trouble and
He thinks that I don't care,
But it's hard when there's often chewing gum
Strategically placed on my chair.

It's the kids you know, they get you down,
Although 'you should't let them beat ya!'
No respect, no discipline, an abundance of tests,
Why did I become a teacher?

Sue A Hill

Is it Time to Make the Killing Field Level?

Moslems fighting for survival
  Despite the overwhelming odds,
Serb Forces, so strong - armed and ruthless
  Against the Bosnian underdogs.

A cherry tree that's in full blossom
  Young bodies in a gruesome state,
Two small Moslem girls once happy -
  A sniper's bullet sealed their fate.

Moslems short of ammunition
  Collect dud shells along the street,
Home-made grenades, crude mortar shells
  A fearsome task, a futile feat.

Well-meaning men in pale blue helmets
  Seek to help relieve the strain,
But people cry for ammunition -
  Not crusts of bread or sacks of grain.

Should they lift the arms embargo?
  World-wide debate goes on and on,
While people are just maimed and murdered,
  Until this dreadful war is done.

Throughout the World in all religions
  So many countries turn to war,
They end up fighting each and other
  Men and women - rich and poor.

Why can't we turn to one another
  Love and kindness try to give?
Treat everyone as sister - brother
  And make our lives a joy to live.

Amy Stone

Justice Pays

He sits up on the chair in court
Looks directly at me
Oblivious to the pain he's caused
To many victims, such as me

The jury wince as they listen to his crimes
Each one orated in full
The man seems to manage a wry smile
As he listens to the things he has done

It doesn't seem to bother him
As the tears flow down my face
It was just another job to him
Another queer erased.

He said he always hated them
They were not the same as him
He felt it was a private war
A war he had to win

His smile is now replaced by tears
As he hears the jury say
They recommend he is jailed for life
And the key be thrown away

He sits there cowering like a child
Not daring to look at me
My tears of pain, replaced by a smile
I know now he will never be free.

Justice pays

Kevin V Jones

The Water Just Ran Away

'The water just ran away this morning,'
Said the harbourmaster about the stranded tanker.
'These things happen at this time of year without warning.'

The sea's breathing, like our own,
Is generally predictable but wayward in the particular.
Tides peak and plummet with syncopated interbeatings,
Forecast from experience and the movement of stars.

Witness the towers in ancient ports
With long-capped telescopes and empty tables
Where men gazed and reckoned and sometimes wondered.
Now computers find if this, then that, within their parameters.

Without their parameters, when winds havoc tidebeats,
Men on quaysides or stranded tankers
Still gaze and reckon and sometimes wonder.
And some November mornings the water just runs away.

Ken Hill

Is This Really Art?

Well, I thought
Is this really a Sunday Supplement?
Asking Us Questions Like That?

Post-Modernism is a Post-Prandial Topic
Along with wet-look raincoats and bedsettees
(That we can just afford at knock-down prices)
I suppose

But is it really art
(They do the colour quite well these days)
Products of a social malaise
I thought
Dishing up the roast.

Veda Dovaston

Union Warns Private Rail Bosses

Management and Union in dispute,
Meetings, deadlock, discussions mute,
Public transport, a must,
Infrastructure, going to rust.

Privatisation causing a bust,
Settlement of demands a must,
Aggressive forewarnings to those who
follow suit,
Weary Commuters to bear the bruit.

Letters of complaint, make no mark,
Policy continues, the same lark,
Fear for the travelcard, but let's see,
A service compatible to the huge fee.

Siobhan Flynn Collins

61

Silos to Rent Suitable for Growing Mushrooms

The Yanks have gone from Greenham,
Their cruise missiles are flown,
They beat their swords to ploughshares
And left us on our own.

The women in their benders
Can sleep in peace at night,
Since their erstwhile defenders
Themselves have taken flight.

No more the dawn death-convoys
Steal, stealthy, through the lanes,
No more the candle protests
Light up the human chains.

The missiles massed for slaughter
Have quit their hostile stance,
The Cold War's had a meltdown:
They're giving peace a chance.

The silent, empty silos
Gape deep beneath the land,
This is the nuclear fallout
They *weren't* built to withstand.

The Treasury's had a brainwave -
They'll let the site on lease,
Recoup a few lost millions:
A dividend on peace.

So come, you mushroom farmers:
Each colonising spore
Prolifically will harness
The rotten spoils of war.

You'll reap a mushroom harvest -
But mushroom clouds no more.

Anne Neuhaus

Famine

He reached out his arm for food -
a limb made of two sticks,
tied together, tightly,
with elastic sheets of skin.

As it extended, the young elbow creaked,
creaked with fatigue at the tiny action
like the rusty hinges
of an aged door.

And before him,
if he cared to look,
his pulse
raised and lowered the rubber sheet.
How long will it continue?

And the long, malshaped fingers splayed out
begging for food,
figured like the horny claws
of an extra terrestrial creature.

Hesitantly they reached out,
Not eagerly
It is not easy to be eager
with hardly the energy
to live.

Katrina Plumb

SIC Transit Gloria Mundi

                    They had a century in tow.
                    Its hearts
                    and minds and human yield.
Germany to Luther; Dutch to tulip field.
The Scots to Knox and Spain took South America apart.
Each madness had its limelight and its cue
and madness had its moment on the stage,
                    but from our point of view
                    we know
they were The Manias of the Age.

                    This is The Virtue of Our Age,
                    Our Hope,
                    This rose; this daily bread.
Millions of words are written; millions read,
and millions swarm across the ashen plain of Europe.
The walls fall down as on and on we plough.
                    Millions rally. It is all the rage,
                    but fifty years from now,
                    they'll say:
It was The Mania of The Age.

John Random

Life is Cheap

I have set fair with them
        for sailing forth, perforce
and utter no complaint
        at their compliance with the forces
within our land for whom
        life is cheap
who regard profit as the sole
        function of employment
and employees as inefficient
        machinery, who see
no contradiction in grain mountains
        and starvation
no guilt in homelessness
        and second homes
no shame in a 'democracy'
        funding despots
no pity in war . . .
        still
no fear of the revengeful dispossessed
        nor of dispassionate nature
Life is cheap
        for whom within our land?
The forces of compliance
        utter no complaint, perforce,
for sailing forth with them
        we have set fair.

Alaric Sumner

66

Mia Gets the Kids Woody Gets the Bill in Custody Battle

Mamma Mia!
Did la Farrow
find it harrow-
in court? Sure,
it was hot. Or
was it just all
more rehearsal
for another
Allen mother-
of-a-movie
that would prove he
was no more than
every next man
of the viewing
public, screwing
up his love-life
taking no wife,
but a lover,
then discover,
like a potion,
deep emotion
for her daughter
when he ought to
keep his bolstered
ego holstered?
Now he's paying;
kids are staying
with the mother;
why'd he bother?

Mamma Mia!

Angela Alba

Judges in the Dock

It makes me proud to be British,
With such a system as ours.
I wish that I could be a judge,
I'll tell you what I'd do.
I'd exonerate the rapists,
Lock up the innocents, especially
The bloody Irish, that's what I'd do.

One must never admit to one's fault.
Women are an inexorable pest,
Influencing eight-year-old girls
To lift up their T-shirts,
Exposing their unformed breasts
To decent, perfectly normal young men.
I'd blame the child, that's what I'd do.

Don't give the women compensation.
Couple of aspirin and they'll be fine.
Don't send the nice men to prison;
Send them to Barbados,
Where all the black natives share their
Passion for unrestricted, kinky sex.
If I were a judge, that's what I'd do.

Oh. Could I be taking the piss?
Why would I be doing that?
When a woman says 'No'.
She doesn't always mean it,
Does she Mr Judge Raymond Dean?
Mr Father Christmas without the presents,
Mr Bloody Jester to the Queen.

Whilst the law continues to run a mock,
It's high time the judges were in the dock.

Sarah Haywood

Murder of the Spirit

What is murder? . . . the word strikes terror,
Life has been taken, no not in error.
Confirmation in Death

Grasp the word, hold it in your mind,
Close your eyes, sit try to define.
Halt and Summarise

Execution is with us, every moment we breath,
Listen to murder, don't try to conceal.
Disguise Revealed

Humanities greed, takes life from many,
In the form of profit, covetous to the last penny.
Humiliation, Degradation

Robbed of your job, loss of your home,
crushing of spirit, yours to bemoan.
Sanity Destroyed

Is this not murder?

Kath Miller

Heroes of the Floating Bomb

It's early morning (Night time somewhere).
These ships pass between
two, huge banks of sand (so it must seem to them)
and meet.

They meet with a *crash*!
Not greeting, but one tears hole in other.
Not yet heroes they grab possessions,
and run (though not all of them).
The men stay behind, as it should be
in things like this.

'The oil was burning a little on the water,
but ten minutes later it was an inferno.'

I think to myself,
What hope could they have,
could anyone have,
trapped on a bomb?

'Seven dead, two missing as officers,
                              are praised.'

Nothing left for me to say.
Those in charge issued a typical terse statement:
Aren't we all heroes of some kind of bomb?

Ben Fielding

Rendezvous With Fear

A man with one leg
goes to vote.

He stands on the edge
of a field,
watching the moon
turn to blood,
head thumping
with his heartbeat
and bullets of sweat.

A cool breath
whispers on his neck,
'You have nothing to fear,'
and draws him across
where men in blue berets
are packing their bags
and zipping their flies.

'It is our secret.'

He feels the rush
as they lift in the air,
scatter the ballots
like confetti
on unhappy brides,
who tremble on the ground,
clutching at their innocence.

"Til death do us part.'

Jane MacNamee

Gathering by the Danube for all the Fun of the Unfair

From Bougainville to Bosnia, Korea to Kurdistan,
The world's oppressed have gathered to right the wrongs of their
fellow man,
The banks of the Danube plays host to the latest UN game,
Searching for a solution to the lands from whence the oppressed
came.

Languages, cultures and world views collide,
The UN has no place to run and no place to hide.
Aztecs seek the return of the Crown of Montezuma and then justice
will be done;
'They took it from us in 1521.'

Bosnian Muslims shout 'Stop murdering children.'
And once again no-one hears them.
Second World War atrocities are on view to all who freely roam,
And old woman in headscarve and heavy coat takes a look and
thinks of home.

Buddhist Monks protest at the persecution of religious believers in
Vietnam,
Surely that is a land that's taken all the conflict it can.
Kurds yell at evil committed against them by the Turks,
And the UN departs, hoping their Master Plan of doing nothing
works.

R Anscombe

Housing Benefit?

Sat on the edge of your bed, the small room seems to
revolve around a single, ill-starred light
bulb - its dark colour is a polluted beach
nobody desires to tread.

To stoned to sleep, to block out everything;
thoughts begin to drink your mind dry, they
seep through the dark like the luminous gleam of the
alarm clock, lit like a cat's-eye, a beacon
for nightmares and dreams, the traffic of sleep.

Caught in the flashlight of your cigarette, the
objects of the room define their place:
man-sized posters make you forget the walls' cold
stare, but the face of the empty fireplace is as
bare as the shelves of the bookcase and your body
fills its weight in the grooves on the bed.

It doesn't seem a week since you last
did this or that; success, or the lack of it,
has left you flat; drained of all colour
and the flush of hope, you spend your days
awaiting your name on a coffee-coloured
envelope beneath a cellophane slat.

Not that I bear any relation to that
Governmental obsession with inflation,
racing along in a car with no windows and only the
mirror for direction; but you, in your drab
room, watching the weather in the light bulb
blow into night, you cannot assume all they
do is right. The politicians will push their
own lives into the following summer and leave you
out of sight.

Nigel Norton

Hurricane Andrew Dashes Hopes of Profit at Lloyds

Cyclonic Hurricanes
Too much raw sugar cane
Fierce dry heat
Unnoticed blistered feet
Whirling winds
Confusive sins
A jittery ticker
A maelstrom
A cacophony
A leprosy of devotion
Of motion
Of emotion
Of Sanctity's demotion
Unfinished.

Ross McCracken

Middle England Hits Back

New Age Travellers with an age old problem;
They face us with grubby kids and sulky dogs
We answer using a thin blue line, a man, an injunction,
So sit back and guess the outcome.

Soundbites of an antisocial threat coming soon to a field near you.
They parked on this farmer's land
We're pretty sure they broke a fence, made a fire
And you know they'll leave an awful mess.

Landowner says: 'I'm ruined.' then goes home
Has a shower, shuts the French doors, watches his news.
Hippy sits in van and says: 'Don't want your rules.'
So is chased, blocked and moved from police zone to police zone.

Landowning MPs pass a law to stand up for our values
Stamp on Travellers - surely not ethnic cleansing?
But stamp on Travellers you stamp on travelling too,
And are you sure you're ready to bury your wheels?

Thank God they're blocking off all the waste land
Keeping out those dangerous hippies and
Protecting your right to your common land;
But obviously not if you are common enough to actually need it.

Common land so precious they let you
Take the dog for a shit on it
But not so enshrined in your keeping
As to let you stand and stay a while.

Steve Chamberlain

Death in the Dark

There was a great outpouring
Of anger, grief and blaming
Of other people.
Thirty-thousand jobs consumed
As thirty-one pits were doomed
To sudden closure.
That was nineteen-ninety-two,
October the thirteenth . . . Whew!

June seventh, nineteen-ninety-three.
Nineteen pits are closed and we
Have not protested
Again. The headline is stark.
For mines, it's 'Death in the dark'.
Communities, built round coal,
Were never given control
Of their livelihood.

The opposite was the aim.
Politicians, without shame,
Forfeit investment
In equipment underground
And a workforce that's renowned.
Is it for profit?
Or could it be out of spite,
To destroy the miners' might?

A headline in verse
Can't make matters worse.

J A Munro

Newspapers' Verdict Over Major Crisis

The judge and the jury
They all did their duty
  And told the PM he was crap.
By being aloof
The press gave him proof
  That disaster would land in his lap.

His absence of clarity
Made for hilarity
  As did his talent to dither,
So after this pasting
(The time he was wasting!)
  His leadership started to wither.

For all had forgotten
The thoroughly rotten
  Predictions the papers had made,
That at the election
The opposite faction's
  Support would put him in the shade.

He carried on ruling
With Heseltine drooling
  Because he had wanted the job;
He'd led the Exchequer
But found someone better
  Who lost the UK a few bob.

We're stuck with him now,
But heaven knows how,
  His support seems remarkably thin,
If it gets any thinner
We'll ask them to dinner
  And sling the whole lot in the bin.

Guy Clapperton

Summer in the City

Six-month sick migraine thick
Yellow sunless sun,
Bloodless disc -
Cloying pause city summer London,
Temple-pressure traffic drones
Like a shattered hive,
Streets lead upon themselves -
Air bleeds -
How can you stand to be alive?

Basement flats, cells of neurosis
and pointless sex.
They move like sad characters in an Orton farce
And hammer their lovers to death.
Summer in the city is a six-month smash and grab:
Overlarge,
Not over pretty:
The deafening zip of body bags.

Andrew Cain

Broken Doll

(Couple jailed for the neglect and murder of their two year old son)

Murder is murder is murder
Whether it's blue or black and white, it's the same to me;
though that shape of repeated evil may have been
branded long ago onto his murderer's flesh, its image is
now, forever, burning into my eye.

Low on the voices of the old commuters
Soft on the newsprint-stained fingers of the travellers
Like empty-head ants, with me, moving nowhere;
Let the blood of the child run through
This short commuter line,
Let him be buried, in grace,
at last in peace, at least in my memory.
Death is not noble or reasonable;
Tears are not practical weapons
for him or for me.

(Ours is a cold and empty race
With no warm heart, no message home;
Ours is a lost and loveless place
This subtle planet, rough and smooth as stone).

Remember him forever
The broken doll;
Lest we forget him, in our senseless haste,
and suffer the pure agony
of forgetting how to feel;
Tomorrow morning's papers
are the worst you've ever read;
The worst is always still to come:
That no-one here remembers him
and misery repeats itself -
No death precludes another, not even his.

Ellie Ling

Sleep Well

Not counting sheep, but counting out the pills;
For the world's ills the soporific cure.
Don't be too sure of certainties tomorrow,
The gift of Morpheus may bring you sorrow,
When melancholy is the pledge for sleep,
And lowering clouds and spirits fail to lift.

'Sleep that knits up the revelled sleeve of care',
Now tangles with despair, designs depression.
The night that once dragged by
Is blanketed, and restlessness smoothed out:
But waking from that halcyon intercession,
The patient finds the day is not so bright.

Over the edge into amnesia:
The frightfulness of doubting who you are
And not quite knowing where you ought to be.
Maybe a lower dose might make it right?
Reclaim the night, ground personality,
Steady the nerves, prevent the mind from blowing?

Brian Mawhinney tosses, turns, and seeks
An expert bolster for a hard decision.
Committee and commission give advice,
And counselled thrice, winnowing
Evidence, he plumps for caution:
A blanket ban being the ready option.

'To sleep, perchance to dream?' Mawhinney wills
The means to end the Sandman's glut of pills.

Mollie Russell-Smith

Sadness as Billy's Leeks Fail to Win a Posthumous Prize

PE teacher weds rugby player.
Cat vendetta, claims owner.
Police saw man in ski mask run from store.
Pair went too far. Youth swore.

Rotweiler killed goat. Car ran into horse.
Hanging baskets repaired. New bins sought.
Tools taken. Bucket stolen.
Car wrecks goal posts. Car wasn't stolen.

Beer bottle hit car. Tax disc out of date.
Landlady is fined for pub's slate.
Karaoke complaints. House could be school.
Cow falls into swimming pool.

Firemen start fire. Vicar joins sewage gang.
Angry man broke window of caravan.
Library under attack. Police van stoned.
More police wanted. Enough post boxes.

Linda France

Miss Sarajevo-Under-Siege

Seventeen year old
Miss Sarajevo-Under-Siege,
in bathing costume and sash,
beams from the stage,
waving flowers.

Her fellow contestants,
beauties all, smiling all,
hold up a banner,
blue on white, in English:

Don't let them kill us

One of the judges
cradles an AK-47.

Michael Lawrence

UN Solution for Disgusting War

I heard the bell toll in my sleep again last night,
My friends said 'Join us, come along and fight'.
Pulled from my bed and pushed to the door,
'Come along' they said, 'we're going to the war'.

They pulled me screaming through the streets and handed me a gun,
I felt a bullet in my back each time I tried to run,
They wouldn't, couldn't, make me fight, I didn't want to kill,
I told them that I would not fight. They screamed, 'You will! You will!',
They made me shoot my brother. They made me shoot my son
And I felt a bullet in my back, each time I tried to run.

The bell tolled for the fighting. The bell tolled for the dead.
The bell tolled in the distance. The bell tolled in my head.
The smell of cordite tortured me and wrapped my mind in pain
But still I kept on shooting, killing again and again.

Steve Smith

Horror Over Child Murder

I read the report in the newspaper, disgusted,
The victim's father is in the camera's eye,
This man will meet the president.
He looks sane but carries the corpse of his murdered child
inside the pocket of his coat,
The corpse is green like swarfega,
The pocket stained and distended.
Over-real instant,
Twisted presentation,
He pulls out the putrid corpse
It's sockets holed like toad eyes,
Thrust in his gaze
The urbane politician reels back at the horror,
Not expecting,
Commiseration's gone.

Stephen Blessett

Village Vigilantes Jailed for Five Years

Village Vigilantes Jailed for Five Years.
Here it is - back page news.
But 'the community is outraged',
For these are 'upright citizens', just 'trying to help the police'.
And the community is 'devastated',
For these are 'law abiding' men.
All they did was to kidnap a 'troublemaker',
A youth of seventeen - a nuisance to the villagers.
They only wanted to dissuade him from criminal activity.
Is that purpose so unreasonable - is that purpose not
understandable?
So they tied him up and threw him in a van and threatened him;
- to cut him with a knife
- to douse him in petrol and set him alight.
Just to teach the youth a lesson, a *suspect* in a wave of crimes.
Is this action so unreasonable - is this action not understandable?
They were just 'genuinely trying to help the police',
The police who were unable to press charges - for lack of evidence.
No lack of evidence for their actions, must we call them crimes?
They pleaded guilty - surely the sentence will be light - *five years*!
And 'the community is outraged',
And 'it's undermined the people's faith in law and order',
For these are 'law-abiding', 'upright citizens', - aren't they?

Sandy Wotton

85

What Poetry Has Come to Nowadays

Two
Petrol bombs
Were hurled
Yesterday
At the office
Of the Tamil
United
Liberation Front
At
Jaffna,
(the principal town in the
Tamil northern province of Sri Lanka)
The explosions damaged
Several windows.

But oh! Petrol bombs
My heart here unwasted
And so much a better target
To be raised again from the ashes!

R G Dowson

You Give Me Fever

(Race hate man in 25ft plunge)

This is where it happened. The bleak film set
of North Birmingham; the white tower blocks
with satellite dishes like cheap earrings.
They chased a black guy up to his flat,

broke in after him, watched him jump.
He walked away on a fractured leg,
but they caught him, used an iron bar
to break his skull. Rain washed the street

back to normality. A week of storms
explains nothing. *How can this happen*?
The newspapers draw a circle around
the victim or the attacker: real people

don't kill *each other*. But violence,
like petrol, is every colour at once.
Nowhere is home; no-one belongs. This district
is the real image of a virtual reality.

A rain of broken glass. A country
that's too insane to offer asylum,
that never gets beyond 'pre' to 'judice'.
Don't shut your eyes and dream it onto

a cinema screen: when the rain stops
and the heat ends, the beatings will go on.
There's nothing to say; warm blood fills
a damaged mouth like sleep. Like silence.

Joel Lane

Squat Thrust

Huddling under a thin blanket on a grimy mattress:
better than being nagged at by redundant parents.

She must get up and walk to keep warm and to stop staring
at the four walls. Her slim body crowned with lank hair,

due to a sparse vegetable and chocolate diet, making
it difficult to resist a drug-induced 'escape'.

Her appearance could be better if she hadn't wasted
another day between the DSS and Housing Department:

Housing Claim still 'being processed'. Social Fund
run out of money. A workman's radio broadcasts a politician:

'Jobless teenagers must not use pregnancy to jump
the housing queue.' No offer of suggested solutions.

'You exclude me from your society, so why
should I obey your rules?' is her response.

She could manage a phantom pregnancy, a few bruises
and an imaginary violent boyfriend to get her a bedsit.

If questioned, a phantom miscarriage could be staged.
All she wants is a place she could call home;

instead of being a victim of a cost-driven bureaucracy.

Emma Barford

No to Treatment

When I am old and grey and full of cancer
When poison's written moving lyrics
And surgeons' knives have answered back,
My body, passive host to all before,
Is now the page for poems of war.

There's purple lines and veins that wax
Creative from my balding brow,
And just inside, beneath dead skin,
The haemoglobin's waging on.

And here, in bed, as drugs transport me
The nurses bring a book of words.
It's not a bible, (He had some mercy),
It's not a will of sorts.
Instead it's just my rites of passage,
An exit from this war of words.

My right hand doesn't function,
So the nurses hold the pen,
Wielding democratic abnegation -
My first choice and my last.

The cancer shouts, 'I'll be your muse
Now write a line and be inspired'.
A gravestone poet I've become,
No suicide, no lemming, me.

'Here lies a weary nobody,
He had a choice and he chose Thee.'

Sophie Eleanor Breese

Borders

The cartographer colours in her maps,
closely following a blueprint culled
from patchy historical records and
politicians' greedy rhetoric.
An enclave here, a safe area there,
a peace zone, a war zone
shaded in the colours of changing
flags of convenience, run up
while you pause for breath,
trying to catch up with a paper visa's
declining currency in a nightmare world
of shifting populations and dying towns.
A different landscape is mapped in your mind's eye,
one of shattered streets and crumbling walls
where a family lies knotted together
with a solitary blanket.
Migrants from obliterated villages
create makeshift homes from stones
blasted out of the streets.
If you don't watch it they will steal
the bulbs from your window box to eat.
Transient streets of shame that
never get drawn by the official cartographer,
whose perverse Utopia does not house the
woman you see singing a lullaby by a little grave
pockmarked by a gunman's bullets.
Or the painfully thin young man shot at the
borders of all this madness by guards
who struggle to keep evacuees from running
like spilt ink out of their stained past.

Penny Simpson

Radiation Beach

Sand grits up a flaccid eye
Earless asses bimbettish in bedizen
Flashed lashes ee-awing like debutantes
Riding the dry waves of protest

Laced white froth flowers into flatulent grey
From the rocks-tear snaps a claw
'Garcon! a toffee apple, Indian tea'.

Yellow saps up from the root of the pen
The crossword left unfinished
Crazed sun smites the face
- *White crab eats red man* -

Christopher Barnes

Linda

I hear you Linda
You're feeling fine
but I'm at a loss without you.
How you inspired me - made me strive for a better life;
not with force but with calm peace
did you show me what is true.

You stood for equality, you loved us all - black or white.
With those gentle arms you embraced me,
you cared for what I said, for what I did.
And now in this cold nadir
I'm empty, vulnerable and really I miss you.

I wake up with a paradox of purpose.
Do I bother with life when you're not here?
Do I pursue those aims you couldn't fulfil?
At one time energy and another despair
but I hear you calling - live your life while it's still there.

Why did you die in that plane crash?
I thought you'd return.
It's been eight months now, but the tears are just the same.
My sister Linda
who taught me how to survive
is dead, and I'm still alive.

I know you're happier even though
I cannot comprehend your delight,
the contentment I'm too mortal to cherish;
but I'm looking forward to that day.
I love you Linda.
My sister Linda who in some sacred sanctuary
looks down on the world and melts my heart.

Fleur Dorrell

Gay Serial Killer on the Loose

A recession weary Britain,
Is excited by the news
Sensational headlines shouting
there is a killer on the loose.

Not just an ordinary murderer,
but, for the papers - so much more.
A shadow from the subculture,
the world the press ignore.

Homosexuals in our front rooms,
the public is aghast.
Psychos in our closets,
Britain is excited - at long last.

The police and populous unite,
to overcome the wall;
Of prejudice and persecution
erected by us all.

When the excitement is over,
We shall creep back to the mundane.
Brush over the subject through dinner,
just carry on the same.

But there is another killer,
And it murders every day
We are executioners through ignorance
and ironically -
label our victims 'Gay'.

Deborah Scott

The Candidate

The good-for-nothing liar
The cheat
The bore

When, rarely, he can do it
He does it with a whore

His head is empty
His ambition without limit

There is but one career for him

Find a safe Parliamentary seat
And win it

Lawrence Harris

England's Decline and . . . Fall

Over the ocean they're having a party
In Boston's fair quarter, where once they spilt tea.
Red shirts have fallen, where once they were mighty
Our football has died in the land of the free.

The manager's cited for losing our dignity
Yet he blames the humidity, and badly cut grass.
I've heard it called Yorktown, a second revolution
Just as the first one, 'They whooped our arse!'

We've held off Armadas intent on invading
Laughed loud at Napoleon, stood firm through a blitz.
Born endless adversities, had pride as a nation
Yet our finest hour was July '66!

They're scattering ashes over our soccer
The world says we're finished, our legend is done.
No Banks, Hurst or Peters is out there to save us
Charlton's too old, and alas Moore has gone.

Many consider our football a simile
The metaphor of all that in Britain's gone flat.
Like recessions, depressions, a wounded economy
The story's the same with ball - or with bat!

Over the ocean the upstarts are cheering
Their victorious roar drowns the cries of our shame.
English Football's no more, now it's history's ended
- If only they'd given Waddle a game!

Carl Sebastian Dines

Spring Time for Women Priests

The Church of England is likely next spring
To ordain its first women priests and bring
Contention to the fore
Once more.

For opponents to the scheme, flying pickets
Sorry, bishops, may be allowed to nip its
Growth in the bud.
Oh God!

Will someone carefully explain to me
Where Equal Opportunities will be
In this plan?
Oh man!

Christianity asks man to love his neighbour.
But at all costs keep woman out of favour.
Holier than thou.
And how!

The Bible tells how the woman Mary
Birthed the Son of God, but men be wary
Lest women claim
In God's name
That this gives womankind the right
To be regarded as equal in the fight
To minister.
It's sinister
That in a Church where before God all are equal
Men dare to call their sisters inconsequential.

C Morris

Tax Write-Off

This year I bought a nuclear submarine.
Well, finished buying one, to be precise.
They are rather expensive and accordingly
I have had to pay for mine a bit at a time,
Over the years since I started work.

Nobody tells you anything, but in my mind
I followed its construction carefully,
And this year, looking at my tax assessment,
I saw that it was conning tower time,
Which I calculated must complete the project,
Apart from a few flags, which are optional.

Last night on TV I watched it sail forth,
From the place where they'd put the bits together.
To another place where they didn't want any of them.
It made me wonder whether I'd perhaps been a bit extravagant.
I can no longer afford to pay for my little house.
But this year I bought a nuclear submarine.

Howard Baker

97

Sonnets for Spielberg

I am a mad cinematic fanatic;
Suppose you could say on the Hook,
Use words like 'Megafantastic',
'Bitchincosmic' and 'Whaddya-look',
- Vocabulary very elastic.
I am crazy for colourful films
About aliens, children and sharks,
Odysseys into exciting realms
With action and special effects
But also with a heart;
Some sentiment inflects
A sense of uncynical joy.
Sometimes it smarts;
But is seldom a ploy.

His latest celluloid super-epic
Is set in the Cretaceous.
The noisy build up has a
Frisson of the outrageous
Full of reptileoid epidemic!
It's based on plain good thinking:
Dinosaurs are *cute*.
Nothing wrong with linking
A modern marketing strategy
(worth a lot of loot)
With beasts of primordial pedigree;
It's kind of like a comeback
A director gone back to his roots,
With huge side orders of greenbacks.

Edward St Boniface

Virgin's Angel

Richard Branson, in jeans and open-necked shirt,
surveys the island of Hydra
where cobbles bubble beneath the sun
and almond blossoms dot the sky.
Here, he will build a luxury hotel
and tourists will walk noisily
along the empty streets
photographing the donkeys
and smiling at women in black
who hang their washing
or whitewash their doorsteps.

Aged four, I lived near the harbour
where bohemians and poets
discussed philosophy
over bottles of cheap wine
beneath wisteria vines.
There Norman Peterson took me on his shoulders
and plunged into the still sea.
I was the rider of a wild sea-monster
and my laughter filled the sky.

This is an island of footsteps:
Branson pursued his fleeing wife
but she would not return.
My father chased my mother's lover
with a ready knife.

The builders will bulldoze
a million memories
and smoky glass windows
will mask the sun -
but my feet will never touch the island again.

Tamar Hodes

Mobile Spy Cameras to Trap London Speeders

Thank you
Sincerely
To the age of innovative technology
For proving
That the video camera serves not only
As a means
To Jeremy Beadle's salary.
That makes me very happy
Indeed.

A revolution
In road safety;
What more
Could the lawful citizen need
To improve his journey?
What more
Indeed.

Well,
Spy cameras
On the railway
To catch a stray leaf,
And drunken driving penalties
That make excuses
For charging a man a grand
For dropping a crisp bag
On the ground;
And what's more,
Roads that don't melt
When summer comes around.
That's what
Indeed.

Lucy Allen

Found Poem

Portrait of the artist as
Researchers trade nightmares in the laboratory of dreamland.
New hitch . . .
550 jobs may go
(Good news for small businesses).
Miners back joint action.

Whitehall defiance:
PM weighs workfare idea
picked out of 3,000 words of waffle.
Right to die unanimously upheld:
Hanged prisoner named
DAF

Derek Frankland

Tanker Disaster Hits Shetland

'Outdamned spot, out I say . . .
All the perfumes of Arabia
Will not sweeten this little hand.'

This lit-tle hand
Counting petro-dollars
Its perfumed chic
       shaikh-owner
Immaculately robed
In spotless white, while

Far to the North
In the land of Thanes
Black damnation
Belches from a broken vessel
(Bubble, bubble, oil-in-trouble)
Blasts a fair island
And murders the sea.

(And on the island's Heath
Dark witches three
Cackle with a sick
      unholy glee . . .)

A tragedy?
Macbeth was a tragedy:
This, methinks
    is very like
       a Crime.

Eugene Leeb

Meteoric Discovery

The Night sky resounded with flashes of light
in blue and red
I missed it I was curled asleep in my bed.

For twenty minutes electric currents
zigzagged the universe unnerving computers
certainties of information become only probabilities
or were lost forever.

Determined to witness the phenomena of nature
upsetting man's carefully laid systems.
His shot at control outmanoeuvred.
I planned to sit at my window.

But sleep was too strong
The activities of the day crowded in
Singleness of purpose was lost
in the infiniteness of minor tasks.
The practicalities of existence
ensuring that the major events go unmarked.

I slept while life exploded all around me.

Kim Hopkinson

103

Lovers Buried to the Sound of Gunfire

They press down, those
black acres of earth, enshrining
the embrace captivated in our minds
not on photographs or film, rather
in fleeting descriptions only
- words from the front where journalists
snatch sentences from their word processed
calculators.

'Two lovers shot dead trying to escape
Sarajevo last week.'

I recall my first embrace, as a young man
in the back of a mini-van.
So unlike the final one enacted for five days
by Bosko and Admira;
Lying dead near a bridge,
Smothering the dust of the road
in an unofficial No Man's Land,
Her arm over his body
in one last gesture of defiance and love.

Now that the valedictory gunfire has faded,
I come to you as a friend might,
with consolation and a vase of imaginary flowers,
crossing my heart with mythical symbol,
stepping out with hope, surely to be unfulfilled.

Paul Whitehead

Intransigence

A pensioner aged seventy nine was fined
$1000 in an Auckland District Court
after police found twenty seven bags
of cannabis in the Mt Roskill unit -
for which she has a lifelong lease.

Judge Mitchell said he was
shocked to discover her convictions
went back sixty years. Vice charges
in 1955, ten weeks imprisonment.
1966 - possession of opium.

Neighbours claimed their dreams
of peaceful retirement were being
shattered. They fear her visitors
will break into their homes.
People feel threatened

one woman said - They come here -
high on drugs, laughing and giggling.
Many fear repercussions - asking
for their names to be suppressed.
Ordered to forfeit $400

disclosed by the police search
stashed in two handbags
Mary Elizabeth Campbell
otherwise known as The Dope Lady
in newspaper headlines said

I'm going to see my lawyer.
But I don't care if I do
have to move. They are such
a miserable pack here and
most of them don't even know me.

Briar Wood

Before the Clock Struck Eight

Were you dispatched quickly?
The paper didn't say,
If anyone had tested the drop
With sandbags and a practised knot.
You once said this was your calling,
What you were put on earth to do,
You couldn't change the verdict
As you saw your duty through.

You were the one who said goodbye,
The last one to look them in the eye,
The last human touch before the
Final kick and then they died.
Now the final judgement has come to you,
You will find out if your conviction was true.
If you have been pardoned
For the job you did on earth,
Then those who should have been allowed to live
Will have surely been pardoned too.

Before the clock struck eight, swiftly
And with dignity from their cell to their death,
Was the code you professed.
Now they are waiting to meet you
They will look into your eyes again,
Will they hold you responsible for
The deeds you did back then?

Martin Holmes

106

Marriage by Arrangement

At first she didn't fight back
Couldn't, anyway
Her English was non-existent.
Married two days and already
His worm had turned.

He'd loved her photograph
But in the flesh she was
The thorn in his pride
A red rag to his bullish side.

And when her scars crusted over
And her aubergine skin
Bleached yellow as the butter
She rubbed it with
He locked her in the house alone
Until her hair grew ashen white
Her heart a shrivelled prune.

She was made to feel at fault when
He scalded her with tea
And then raped her to
Impregnate her to
Prove he was a man.

Then came the night he whipped her
Before sleeping the sleep
Of the Just.
And she put paid to him
Cremated him, licked
Her wounds by his funeral pyre.

She never fought back
Couldn't, anyway he
Was twice her size.
Married ten years before the
Worm in her turned.

Annie Moir

Convoy of Joy

Travni-Vitez
An unknown valley
Until in our safe homes
We see images of despair
Held in it's shadow.
Over the hills
People whose need held them captive
Wait for the convoy of joy
To bring a promise of freedom.
Time held it's breath
As hope faded
Blood flowed
The crimson artery of a
Dying town spilling over
Mingling it's
Salt tears with the dusty soil
Their hope torn away
By the bullets of hatred.

Sheila Badham

Lost Motorist is Driven Mad

Stuff paled out,
to give a vista
that was strange,
macabre as something cooked-up.

Afraid I was losing
my senses I held
onto the steering wheel,
blood froze in my veins.

My head began to ache,
I opened my map:
nothing in it helped
me find out where I was.

I let the engine stall.
Shutting my eyes
I hoped it was a dream,
prayed it would end.

Nothing changed:
the landscape was
a skull that grinned
at who I was.

I was on my own,
distraught and very scared,
I didn't know
which road I'd followed,

where I was, was weird.
I leaned back,
tried to think,
I couldn't stop madness from coming.

Peter Cardwell

New Vote Over Rope

There is renewed hope
for a new vote
on the rope
for the yes vote
for the no vote
altogether it's a
no hoper
free thinkers
look to justice
terrorist killings
and child murders
the sympathy speakers
plead their objections
call a referendum
no contest.

Sylvia Ellen Smith

Gone Shopping: Reflections on Christmas 1989

Christmas communist regime
Party's gone shopping, very keen
That's the key to staying in power
Don't stop the shoppers' happy hour

Seems the same the whole world over
East Berlin, Prague, Moscow, Dover(?)

It's no coincidence I think
That the proles kick up a stink
Just as Christmas rears its head.
Communism, so called, is dead

Down comes the city-splitting wall
Goods aplenty for one and all
Hey, East Berliners, here's some cash
Spend! Spend! Spend! Go on, be rash

Politburo soon all resigns
They didn't spot the Noel signs
BBC: Is eet democracy thart you chaps need?
Leave it out mate, it's Christmas greed

Need a Teddy for 'Our Kid'
Need a Telly for Comrade Sid
Want 501s more than the vote
Western correspondents, take note

So the doctrine of Karl the Marx
Stands aside for Marks and Sparks
Erich Honicker has had his day
Followed Stalin; it didn't pay

Central Planning couldn't fill the stocking
So the Eastern Bloc's gone out shopping

Kelvin Mason

City's Gays Refuse to Panic Over Selective Serial Killer

Next time you pick up a guy
Just might be your last
But you say
       it's just another risk to take.

There's homophobia, party raids
HIV, full-blown AIDS
Now serial killing
       - what's so new?

Society will not take our side
We're the ones who need to shout
But we say
       accept these things, we're only gay.

We breach the peace each time we kiss
Our family lives are all pretend
Serial killing
       - what we're worth?

Are you ever Glad to Be?
Will you ever march in Pride?
Stand up and say
       no more of this!

Let's be angry, let's be proud
Let's claim out loud our right to live
Serial killing
       Not on us!

Juliet Wilson

La Dolce Vita is Finally Over

Given immunity from prosecution,
Politicians wait.
Past corruption without retribution,
Judges investigate.

Operation Clean Hands confronts the maligned
Legacy of illegality.
Tear out the pockets so richly lined,
Legislate morality.

The kickbacks,
Kickback.

Creative destruction of the political system,
Partyocracy dismembered.
Civic communities with greater freedom,
Democracy remembered.

John Tobin

Cliff Top Hotel Set to Slip Over the Edge

It was a time when . . .

The grass grew thin,
calamities exploded on remote areas,
waves crashed on suburbia,
a surfer soared over the rooftops.
Thunder clouds were stacked
ten thousand feet high

No one cared less,
least not the newspapers
vying with column acres
of saucy bimbos spanking bums
and conversations taped between
royal nobodies between expensive junkets.

All were mad or driven mad
by babble rising the depths . . .
While a surfer soared over the rooftops . . .

Frank Questing

Cot Deaths

Babies can be killed by their dreams
They dream they are back in their mothers' womb
Where there was no need to breathe

Incredible agony is felt by all
The heartache that's caused when a young life dies
is unequalled by any world news

What injustice from God to take a child
When there are far more deserving of death
Perhaps they go to a better world where there is no need for breath

Elizabeth Munson

116

Madmen Martyrs and Crazy Cults

Waco ashes
still warm   dappled with bone
what's going on?

Cauterised
another inferno scarcely scalds
sucking pasta as newsreaders spurt disasters

Empathy
entombed lies stiff and chilly
stuck to the pan like cold tagliatelle.

Bloated with photos
dying children   flies on their eyelids
Sunday supplement pain grows anodyne.

Full to bursting
not even the shocking touches
a family laughing   the last wild orchids.

Diana Gittins

World of Opportunity

She's landed a job at the United Nations
she'll be spending some time overseas,
to further her global aspirations
and speak on behalf of the world's refugees.

She's overcome some stiff opposition
to end up in this, her latest position.

I didn't see the job advertised
was it open to competition?
Or on a nod and a wink advised
to tempt a personal ambition?

Packing them in and stating her case
flying around all over the place.

What was the recruitment procedure
which brought her this meaningful role?
Is it really true no-one could beat her,
with three million stuck on the dole?

To Mozambique on a high profile mission
pictured in Newsweek and on television.

In hot dusty places she'll keep her composure
gadding about in a four-wheel drive
making the most of the media exposure
an unsalaried post but I think she'll survive.

A caring expression can boost popularity
clouding the memory of past vulgarity.

As flashpoints increase and the outlook worsens
the privileged few will carry the flag
waving at millions of displaced persons
then off back to Heathrow and home in the Jag.

It really is excellent public relations
skirting around the United Nations.

Steve Woollard

Invalidity Benefit Could be Taxed

There is talk of taxing the sick
the illest of us all
Or are they?
What about the little men in large suits?

They sit around smoking, smiling and say
'Got it! Pick on the weakest of weak
Tax the meek
The least likely to resist
Isn't it obvious - no-one will care?
There was a march for the miners,
the pits closed
and who was there?
No-one.
It's always the same. We get the blame
but remain unscathed in the end
then spend, spend, spend
on military, macho things.
The black hole of Wednesday swallowed millions -
We'll make up for it this way - make them pay.'

And such is this place, where the Government governs
by way of self-imposed divine right.
All public-school, money, male and white
what does it know of the people's plight?

Nothing, But probes the further possibilities
of further exploitation,
as there's no agitation, no education, no organisation
We have this sick situation
with judges insane, politicians inane,
the poor in pain.
Who to blame?

Michelle Dunne

Murdered Lovers' Bodies Disappear in the Night

A modern-day
Shakespearean play
Has ended in a mystery;
Love united Serb and Moslem,
Now in death no-one can find them.

Once they lay in No-Man's Land,
Killed while running hand in hand
From Sarajevo
Land of war
The victims of religion's law.

But overnight they each were stolen,
(One to Serb
And one to Moslem?)
So in death they separate,
Killed in love
By those who hate.

Jonathan Lloyd

Murder Mystery Jigsaw

Putting aside the newspaper,
I turned to the box of pieces
With the magnifying glass and Holmes
Silhouette on the cover.

You are the investigating officer.
Discover the murderer
In the comfort of your own home.

Sort out all the pieces,
Build the outline of the case,
Sift the evidence with a methodical mind,
And the picture will fall into place.

But there was only an hour before the tv news,
So I chose to ignore the rules,
Picking up pieces with a logic known only to me.
Forcing them to wed each other in a murderous mosaic,
Until I convinced myself it would do.

And what lay there on the table top
Was a picture of a High Court judge,
And a group of four security guards.
All with slightly confused looks on their faces,
Staring out at what must have been
A large crowd of angry people.

And in the bottom left hand corner,
So you might easily have missed it,
The perforated body
Of a dead woman lay awkwardly,
With hands, and eyes, and mouth
Open, as though pleading,
Or appealing.

Sonny Peart

122

James Bulger 1991-1993

Only two years old
And yet has filled a page
In the tragic history
Of our country.

One moment happy, laughing.
A tiny soul,
Carefree as a bird,
Then dead.
The world joins with his parents
And weeps.

Weeps not only for them,
For James,
But for the parents of those
Who closed the eyes,
Turned out the shining light
Of one so innocent and pure.

They too will lose their sons,
Who, merely babes themselves,
Rudely took on the role -
For sport, mastery, experiment -
Of executioner.

There have been
And sadly, will be more
Like James.
So how can we instil
Into our fellows
That we must preserve
The gift of life?
A gift so precious
That no mortal may destroy.

Elizabeth Spencer

Here's Looking at you Kid

Daniel looks at Rebecca,
her eyes flit from wall to wall;
shocked, horrified, reluctant to rest her eyes anywhere.
The newscaster reels off the other headlines -
men on Mars, the flooding of London -
but Rebecca, now shaking, can only think of her friends,
murdered by this man-made plague.
Orwell's 84 was in full swing, and had been for a while.
Even when the 'free' West pointed fingers at the East,
Big Brother was growing in strength.
Daniel looks at Rebecca, and takes her hand,
she lets her gaze drift beyond the window-pane.
The sun decides enough is enough for one day,
and leaves the half-baked city to search for answers
in a blood-red sky.
The film of smog below their flat, reeks of death.
The candles on Daniel's birthday cake, continue to burn,
as if mourning; weeping wax drips upon white icing.
It was an exiled agent, formerly with the FBI,
who revealed all to a wanton journalist late, last night:
AIDS was conceived in a test-tube (along with a cure -
for executive use, only),
they claimed they 'simply had to attempt to control,
the population-explosion somehow'.
Rebecca looks at Daniel,
still his hands hold hers,
'Happy Birthday', she says through a hoarse voice.

Karl Powell

Untitled

a girl who was no angel strode this mortal plane
as such she could not be absolved of blame
empowered to make judgement, or comment as inept
or just, the feeling crept,
was misspent on an orifice of office
now finding its credibility to sustain,
impossible, and lent to reason sent
from the logic of the branches in a cuckoo's nest bent

'Justice is a Travesty' wrappers on chips flapped
the heat within now rising, barely trapped
on their behalf the 'People's Gob' spat vitriol with hate
in consensus at the horror of this fact
had teenage lust of reason sapped or truly drained
the discernment of this youth so callow brained?
when invested with a trust was he compelled to fall from grace
was it in his nature as a man?
'except for ma all girls are whores', all holes to be explored'

and was she really teasing, like young girls really do
when eight-years-old to someone twice their years plus two
to be so bold, blessed, with a talent to allure
nay surely she just mimicked the images she saw
and going through the motions was it just another case
of unravelled truths too complex or wisdom's view too base
wielded, seemingly, is this democratic tool
to the will of the flesh
in the hands of a fool

Roger Greenslade

125

Nine London Hospitals Earmarked for Closure

The advisors of the Government tell us
London's hospitals are scattered here and there
And that they should be crammed together
In an office block with room to spare

They tell us that this would be efficient
The truth of this I cannot see
Any savings to be found
Are normally lost in bureaucracy

And the precious thing that will be lost
Which has taken many years to build
Is the dedication of specialist teams
And the promise they have fulfilled

Who really are these advisors
Do they even talk to nurses and doctors
Or are they merely grey money men
Reflecting their Parliamentary sponsors

Richard A Lapworth

Tory says Capitalism Wrecks People's Lives

At last, the unpalatable truth
Out of the mouths of baby Tories,
We knew it all along of course
But lapped it up like fairy stories,
While the world's slit up a treat
By gangsters in designer best
Who slip the knife in with a smile,
Expect us all to be impressed
By how they really won the war
Tore the wall down, made it safe
For investors then to speculate
How to profit from the waste.
We know, of course, the bad guys lost,
Or at least they changed their tune
The average Apparatchik
Is just as happy to consume
As dissidents who dared to dream
Of colour in a world gone stale,
Where are they now? Where were they then,
Some in exile. Some in jail.
And where are the dissenters now
Who'll rally to a different cause
Wake us from the tyranny
Of slavery to market laws.
One cannot be both poor and free,
Poverty will bind the soul
As sure and tight as dogma will
This truth must be forever told
One cannot be both poor *and* free.

Michael Conaghan

Wild and Beautiful

Gone are the days of miracle and wonder;
Here are the ways of insecurity and blunder.
Disappeared are the moments of patience,
Replaced with seconds of hurried worry,
Over those who have no control,
But still control our daily destiny.
There's glass on the streets,
And violence in their heads.
Someone else's possessions,
Now grace their beds.
Dogs on the prowl
Howl from the pavement.
It's no surprise I'm no longer at home.
The sun has set, the day is over;
Seems another chapter has closed.

Kevin Bolt

No Further Room for Improvement

There's no further room for improvement.
There's no Superperson in sight.
After millions of years
Steeped in blood, sweat and tears
Our genes have at last got it right.

There's no further room for improvement.
Mankind has arrived at its prime.
Selection completed,
All hope is defeated
And God has been wasting His time.

There's no further room for improvement.
We've done all the changing we need.
No part one can name
May be given the blame
For our violence, corruption and greed.

There's no further room for improvement?
That's what the Professor has said,
So we'd better transcend
This genetic dead-end
And work on our spirits instead.

Jean Hayes

Hazards

Lakes are always eerie, ghostly, strange
A demon could lurk in the dark secrets
Of the inky depths
Or tragedy strike near the illusory calm
Of peaceful stillness
And yet I cannot wait to drown
In the deepness
Of your eyes

Baubles from fruits of mother earth
Bright, charming adornment
Or evil talisman
Not costly
Unless death is the price
And yet I avidly drink
The venom
From your lips

Pamela D Hewitt

Bloodstock

The Lipizzaners of Croatia
(Stables worried about bloodstock pay for 150 Lipizzaners to be
transported through the war zone)

First class passengers
hurtling through the war zone
- bloodshock.
Never mind the people
- we're bloodstock,
making transport history.

We've been saved before
from the ravages of war,
and suffered circus tricks, viruses,
carriage driving competitions.

The horsebox train
convoys down scattered lanes
avoiding ambush.
But we know no fear,
our good breeding is clear
- the Andalucian strain
shows.

And we think of those
who are left behind,
a symbol of the city.
And you think what a pity,
but then people are so vain,
to inflict us with their pain
- bloodshock.
Never mind the horses
- they're bloodstock,
making military history.

Julie Callan

131

Machine-Gun Gang Brings Terror to New Yorkers

In this country they stand in line to catch buses
In LA they stand in line to buy guns
US drive in and drive thru convenience
Now a new drive by bullet spray product
Product of the sickness of guns
Colt 45 - beer or pistol?
New language accepted from guns
Sleek .38s, Magnum power, oh yes Uzi,
Glamorise the names, make them sexy;
Machined metal mutilators - yes guns
They're splattered guts, shattered cartilage,
Splintered bones, shredded tissue
A wasted life is so romantic, yes guns.
A man down means depressed in this country
But there it's a cop shot through with a gun
But I feel down as I survey the situation
Is this nation so obsessed with guns?

The police wear them visibly - guns
The gangs use them visibly - guns
Criminals point them visibly - guns
Movies, TV all make visible - guns

In the classroom school kids fighting with guns
Home protectors, vigilant neighbours with guns
US violent death rates means guns
One dead every half hour means guns

You're running in circles
With no end to the endless circle
of killing and maiming that
spiral ever upward of
the precision rifled barrel of a gun

Nicholas Mills

Good (?) Fortune

South coast man wins two million on the pools.
Is he happy? How's he spending it? Let's ask him.

Well, I'm going to get married. We'll honeymoon in Greece.
I'm going to fund the education of my nephew and niece.
Buy a couple of cars - will Mercedes do?
New fittings for the derelict house we'll renovate and move into.
Gold-plated taps on showers and sinks.
Stick a bar in one corner and stuff it full of drinks.
Hmm - Axminster or Berber - what do *you* think?
Oh, don't bother, just give us both.

She wants a kitchen with every appliance.
I want a wardrobe furnished uptown.
Mustn't forget a security system,
Don't let the burglars get you down.
Boom boom. Little joke there.

Home entertainment controlled by one panel
with Dolby surround on sixty four channels
of TVs, computers, videos and hi-fis -
A feast for the ears and a treat for the eyes.
Program your pleasure as quick as a flash.
Reckon I'll get a discount for cash?
Worth asking, I suppose.

Invest the rest in gilts and you won't have any.
Guilt, I mean. And no more fear.
Just everything you want and a salary of one hundred and
twenty five grand a year. Gross, give or take a grand.
Yes, of course I'm happy. Especially when I've cash in hand.

Oh Good.
South coast man wins two million on the pools.
Bastard.

Richard Cray

Trial and Terror

Is it because your embarrassed
To speak up when the bullies in the bar
Are lying and cheating and bragging
About their female conquests, most of which are imagined
And on the bar lays a headline, 'Mum raped in a car'
And the article says, 'In broad daylight'
More than one, there must be something amiss
Does that mean they'll get eight months instead of only six
What the hell does it matter if it's in the darkest of night
For the crime that steals from a woman
What God gave her to create life

But somebody did this, this despicable thing
Even the animals have respect, for all female offspring
But somebody did this, and try if you can
You have got to accept that, that somebody was a man
I'm not going to stand here as a man and try
To imagine the horror of losing more than your life
To be defiled by an evil trait of man
Who is then judged by his brother, who can only share his pain

So all you female voices listen, heed the honour in your soul
The judges of this evil act must be women through and through
You do not judge a murderer with the evil doer's friend
So join together all of you and bring this lie to an end
All I can say in my own male defence, is that somewhere in my life
There must have been sitting at the bar, a mother or a wife
Who taught respect and love, for this alien life force, our other half

That beautiful being that is female, who touched my soul with love
Must start the fight now, perhaps banning page three.
A deed that would give a lot of men, the reason that it would give me.

David Germain Clark

134

Our Man in the Cabinet

Only women bleed
which is Nature's penance
A flood maybe
A trace perhaps
Some tension, some pain
Try tell Mr Hunt about
Endometriosis

Only women bare
which is Nature's gift
A boy maybe
A girl perhaps
Some contractions, some pain
Try tell Mr Hunt about
Epidurals

Only women understand women
Which is Nature's way
A sister maybe
A friend perhaps
Some compassion, some pain
Try tell Mr Hunt about
Empathy

Only Mr Hunt is male
Which is Nature's choice
A husband maybe
A lover perhaps
Some chivalry, some chauvinism
Try tell Mr Hunt about
Equality.

Jayne Singh

The Frozen Wasteland

Sitting, waiting in the ice cold wastes of some indescribable world,
Waiting, waiting, waiting,
Life suspended in time awaiting another's intervention.
Waiting to complete yet another cycle of regeneration.
Life cycle. The maelstrom of light and colour ever spinning.
Separate yet unified
Then silence.
Faith, hope and the beginning of another generation lie within me.
Waiting.
For other's speculation.
And deliberation.
Just waiting to end the silence.
Property and chattels are ephemera; nuances of the physical.
There are no such limitations in the infinite.
Life cycle.
Simply waiting for the donee to accept the dance must begin again.
No property in that simple act
of creation.

Karen Hyman

Number Problem Crunched

So Fermat's last theorem is
proved
After three hundred years
Of mathematical tears
And fears
It may not be true
Now we know
x to the n plus y to the n is never
z to the n
when n is an integer
greater than two
One question remains
When Fermat claims
He has a proof
Too large for his page
Is it a joke?
Has he been laughing
For three hundred years?

Phelan Jumawan

Auntie Contemplates Cosmetic Surgery

'Auntie contemplates cosmetic surgery,' Mum mumbled to Dad,
as another herd of animals smashed through the barricades,
a pulsating mass of limbs and heads, eyes bulging
with manic desire, desperate and determined
to start ripping up, tearing up their prey. And

as we watch with morbid fascinated horror, the self-appointed,
self-governing, self-serving police force begin
their nightly tour of duty, daubing their secret signs
upon front doors, so the animals know which way to run.

Above the howling wails of triumph comes
the screaming sirens supping molotov cocktails whilst
lounging amongst the flames. From which emerge the ghouls
who stand around baiting and prodding the animals,
assimilating every action for tomorrow's publication's
of lies: 'Exclusive economical truth!'

I opened the door and watched the two-eyed, twenty
headed millipede gallop towards me barking out their
delight at the scared scuttling of their prey, who soldered
shoulder to shoulder, screamingly searched for safety
in the animal's lair. 'Come on,

join us,' it hissed as it passed. I stood and watched
it's tail disappear around a corner, after those who
dared to follow a different culture, a different
dress code, to have different looks. Auntie will be safe
now after cosmetic surgery, to bleach her skin and
westernise her features. She will be safe, but like me, now,
no longer exists.

Lisa Donoghue

Closure of Pits

It's not the end of it.
Slow slow as unpumped water
coaldust - black in blacker
darkness, to reclaim its rights,
rises towards mountain-high
surface, come up with it all
those died down there, crushed
to pulp-geology while winning
compressed power made damp
offshore island to once-empire.
Now, it is all over, now all is
clear - they died for nothing.
Now, blackness in blackness held,
they come again to choke thought,
to drown the blind, to drag down
to take their place where they
belong those who pretend they
forgot or never knew the price
of coal, the bill now coming
up from wet-tomb darkness so
long overdue.

Steve Sneyd

139

Major Stands by the Chancellor as Devalued Sterling Leaves ERM

'*Old Lady of Threadneedle Street is Raped!*'
So shout the banner headlines round the town.
'*Gang went for Bust!*' '*Her Chest has been reshaped!*'
'*Herr Bundes Bonk Found with his Trousers Down!*'
Her blue-eyed sons both hang their heads in shame,
And friends make little effort to defend 'em.
While Huns were fast devaluing the dame,
They had their eyes upon La Referendum.
Admitted, she's a pretty French coquette,
The daughter of the dying Mitterand.
The blue-eyed twins' hearts pound for her, and yet
She won't say Oui, but nor will she say Non.
   These greying suitors, John and Norman, squirm.
   So torn, they cannot even utter, 'ERM . . . '

Michael Ward

Man is Raped in London Underground Train Attack

So it has come to this:
equality will get you
buggered at
London Bridge,
and men can feel
the frisson of the
rapist's tool, and fear
unlighted
passageways
and late-night
tubes just like
their sisters have
for countless years
since men
invented ravishment
from lust and hate.
A sign of the
times, my friends:
The Rape Suite's
Uni-sex.

Jeremy Gibson

Ancient Sites Protected from Army's Tanks

There's a most
del-i-cate balance
if
you
have
heavy
mighty
military
machinery
marauding
menacingly:
Crack!
monumental
archaeological
de-cons-truc-tion.
Would Salisbury Plain be the same?

Peter Poole

Billy the Kid Blows it

aw Billy now what you done
going in heavy dropping them bombs
smacks a little of the age old style
trouble at home - give 'em blood for awhile

you was gonna be different turn it around
for the women and the blacks and the poor downtown
for the rest of the west was a glimmer of light
a swing to the left not a shuffle to the right
a little more chance for a little less war
no more cowboys quick on the draw

but here you go playing tit for tat
missiles fired at Saddam's Baghdad

retaliation for a failed assassination
you don't even wait for the United Nations

big guns blazing blam blam blam
just like good old Uncle Sam
it might put muscles on your image back home
but the suffering in Iraq goes on and on

and there's people asking questions as well they may
why some despots geddit and some just get away

hey Billy weigh up the damage
(an eye for an eye and one on the image)
c'mon Billy
we don't want all that again
leave the duels to the cowboys
the future needs men

Cath Staincliffe

Right Royals

Yorks Rule Out Marriage Reconciliation (Telegraph)
Shame, and such a lovely couple
Yorks Agree Terms of Legal Separation (Times)
How Jolly Civilised
I'll Never go back to Andy (Mirror)
How sad what will Her Maj think
Fergie : It's Really Over (Mail)
Yawn
Fergie's One Million Parting Gift (Express)
Well she deserves it
Fergie's Two Million Kiss Off (Today)
Why I'd give her my money
If I had some.

Danny Herbert

144

Getting Away With Terror

I am God with my gun
the shot rings out
lost upon the wind
the crumpled soul falls laughing to his knees

Low clouds that speak of god
rushing by
reflect in his still eye:
his mother's once new born,
dead at thirty three.

James Douglas-Hamilton

Lovely Jubbly

'Lovely Jubbly' was all you had to say
The day after the sisters you helped put away
Were set free.

A comedy actor with an OBE
Is more newsworthy it seems to me
Than justice.

Why were these new twists ignored?
Past its sell by date? You just got bored?
Of kisses,

And diary entries, that had sworn to kill
The wife, of the man, that she loved still.
Now that's news!

So we weren't told of the homeless man
Or the descriptions of the girls that ran
Away that day.

Why let good honest truth spoil a story
Let's talk about TV, let's talk about Tories
And actresses.

So 'Lovely Jubbly' is the news today
Atrocities, embarrassments brushed away
'In the Sun.'

Steve Dyche

Clinton Hails Strike as Success
Six Dead as Missiles Miss Iraqi Target

In the households of the Western World
The word may be 'success'
Like the outcome of a football game
The latest movie screen test
Bombs duly meet their targets
And we watch the credits roll
If it's all designed to keep the peace
Then what's the real goal?
As we all look to our leaders
And they to the US
We rely upon discretion
To minimise distress
We feel better for the comfort
When a tyrant meets his fall
And there's nothing like a victory
To keep you walking tall
We live in a democracy
We know it's for the best
The teams have been decided
And it's us versus the rest
The latest air strike may have fallen short
On a couple of targets
But the mission was accomplished
And with that we'll disregard it
To the civilians in the shelters
Or hovering 'round hospital beds
It wasn't us who started it
So just watch where you tread
There's no excuses for your actions
It's just outright terrorism
And now you'll count your casualties
'Cause it's us that makes the decisions.

John Scannell

Howard to Approve Longer Police Baton

Lengthening the stick
To shorten the criminal crop
We stand to stare in admiration
At our harvest feats
Which leave a stubbled earth
Concealing cancerous roots,
Mocking the cure
For our baleful afflictions
And ready to accept
The fallen seed
Which flies, unheeded
By a baton, that only flails,
Yet fails
To beat down the hatchers
Of our future harvest feast.

Stephen Cartmell

Shock Horror Probe

Why am I suddenly
Impervious to the screaming headlines
That once deafened me?
Where are the obligatory feelings
Of hate, rage, outrage, revulsion . . .
Now, perversely, I direct my anger, my hostility
Towards the baying, frothing hack-hounds of the newsroom -
The frenzied scribblers with the self-righteous gleam.
Am I the only one who fears these moral guardians of the new age?
(I imagine their ancestors -
'Our man at the inquisition' or
'Special correspondent with the Torquemada Tour')
Am I the only one who fears a society based on truth and justice
- Tabloid style?

Beverley Ashworth

149

Trustees Rule on Baby Lord Moynihan

The Third Lord Moynihan of Leeds
is dead. A 'Tory bore' succeeds
his brother to the House, unless -
to help a Member in distress -
trustees fulfil a nation's needs
and find a masseuse who concedes
Daniel, her son, as his : God bless
  The Fourth Lord Moynihan

And God bless any man who leads
a life of luxury, on proceeds
of fraud, in exile; others press
their case to come, and I confess
to wishing us the one man less:
  The Fourth Lord Moynihan

Ian Walton

150

In the PM's Pocket

The Tory Party's pockets
Are full of wondrous things,
Of cars and cash and sealing wax,
Of cabbages and strings.

Strings that pull the wool over eyes,
And strings that pull in votes,
Strings that look like old school ties
For hanging old Deep Throats.

Every pocket's filled to bust
Except the inside breast;
Where the Tory heart should be,
Alone a wallet rests.

But now they're breeding special pigs
That have a human gene,
So every Tory can have a heart
And become a human being.

Conservatives can soon converse
And talk of many things -
Why their blood is boiling hot,
And whether pigs have strings.

Simon Bourke

News in Brief

A tiny paragraph
Schoolgirl murdered
Aged fourteen.
Stabbed to death
Walking dog in Grimsby.
A diligent and popular girl.
And worth far less space
Than the just caught
Charismatic
Double spreaded
Drug smuggler,
With the boyish grin.

James Dallas

Armed Women Soldiers in Ulster

A woman lays her babe to rest
And shades it from the sun
The baby-sitting father pleads
As she takes up her gun

'Don't do it love, there's other ways
To end this thing you know,'
But as a tear forms in his eye
She turns dry-eyed to go

'Your dinner's in the oven,
I've fed the dog and cat,'
He indicates the child asleep
But she's no time for that

And silently an old man
Recites the rosary
He hopes that this will change things
And one day they'll be free

She scans the street emotionless
The madness strikes her eyes
A sniper darts behind a wall
A blackness fills the skies

They poise, they aim, a shot rings out
Eyes meet, remembrance fresh
Recalls a love once young and new
A bullet bites soft flesh

He runs to clasp her in his arms
Red tears trail down her face
A child screams out its heartache
Tears merge with baby lace

And silently an old man
Recites the rosary . . .

Jean Gray

Lasting Lure of the Stones

Once strong, once proud, once commanding all
Unknown in origin
But certain in purpose
Attacked on all sides, by old certainly,
But also by new.
Harried, beaten, hurt
Huddled into open field
Hopelessly strangled, by subtle spiteful means.
An island in hostile seas
Beckoning in forlorn hope
To children whose only sword is wrecked
Constantly kicked about
Gathering wretchedly small
At certain times
Guided by ancient sciences
Loved, cherished, nurtured,
A symbol, The symbol
Ancient, yet renewed
By dwindling, yet existing care.

Cameron McIntyre

Villanelle: The Pro-Porn Feminist

Surely it's because she's only human
she has a penchant for surrealist love.
She ain't necessarily just woman.

She likes some spice with sex (like cummin
in a curry - the most essential stuff.)
Surely it's because she's only human.

Taking someone close to her bosom
she handles them just a trifle rough.
She ain't necessarily just woman.

Faced with hard-core porn, she's fuming
at the fact there's nowhere near enough.
Surely it's because she's only human.

Jealously, she guards her own position
against censorship - by talking tough.
She ain't necessarily just woman.

Like it or not, polite public opinion
may one day change and cease to disapprove.
Surely it's because she's only human.
She ain't necessarily just woman.

Dymphna Callery

Disartened Fights to Turn the Tables

Aides stressed that His appeal
to bedrock stonewashed Tory values
- spelt v-a-l-u-e-s - steaming
in the concrete matter of the three-arsed fables
- spelt w-r-i-t-i-n-g -
was Noah tempting us back to the ark
like horses on our straight hack-it courses
away from trendy analytical skills
to mummified annual liturgical smells.

Two by two we held each others hand
for, living singly, filing through the patterned stables
there was no wish in our hearts at least
to die of ignorance.

Tanya Gupta

Roads

They shuffle out of silence, scuff fine sand,
Grey men sandblasted out of blasted stone,
Eyes tracing each defeated footstep, minds
Blunted by terror, endless falling fire.

They stop in silence, queue into the unknown,
Following the orders and the brandished guns;
A cold wind scourges, far horizons burn,
A desert is seeded by long rain of bombs,
Alive with mines, gaping with open graves,
Defeated armies dig out nightmares here

For those who sleep, their faces iced by fire,
Bodies drenched black by napalm, mouths ajar,
Grimacing in final, never-ending screams,
One charred arm, signpost, poised, points into nowhere.

They sit in silence, the traffic jam begins
Where the first rocket fell, and never ends;
This stillness car-park for a holocaust
That locked retreat in fire, that bled and burned
Until all skin was ash, all metal rust,
All thoughts of victory crushed to grains of sand

That drift to mask and to unmask the dead,
Denouncing all who travel these same roads.

Martyn Halsall

Any Headline Any Paper

Under stars of fusion bright,
In the station platform's light,
Can be seen the neutron bomb.

R F Hitchcott

For Mercy Read Murder

In the cell wrench planks my head shall rest on no more.
Clench cold cold bars, stifling hope.
See the priest, fatherly face, noiseless tread.
Hear rites performed, the last communion.
Prisoners banging, like rolling drums.

In the midst of haunted shadows,
In amongst awaiting onlookers,
Feel pounding, booming, deep heart beats.
See men my frame manhandle.
Funeral-pace feet, lingering body.

Here I sit encircled by eyes,
Blue eyes, brown eyes, sad eyes, grim eyes.
Brow feels numb, sweat staved.
I haven't danced for my captive audience.

My God see his hooded head.
Dark hands near, final death knell.
Feel cap upon my crow hair.
All sins flashing in front of me:
Innocence, my ultimate penance.

S R Ilett (16)

Shame and Pride in a Tragic Farewell

shame and pride in
a tragic
farewell, shame he proclaimed before
he died, taking no pride in this his
last act. The shame was not
about dying, he wanted to say, but

about dying in that way: agitated beyond belief, devoid of
dignity, dissolute, and yet
he knew that what was about to come, though
disconcerting,
bore little resemblance to death as expunging life, it

was more of a chastening imposed on the fact of his creed
or colour or any other *imperfection* they cared to quote.
But there was

pride, of the ominous type, in the way
he solemnly passed away, how he was put to rest later,
how his memory persisted in staying
alive, magnetically drawing
those who mourned his absence, even those

who bid him farewell in silence,
from afar.

Isabel Sukan

Blue Men in Pleasure Boats

*(In memory of Julie and Stephen Moles who
died tragically in the frozen Potomac fishing
pond at Gunnersbury Park, West London on
17 February 1991. Julie, aged thirteen, gave
her life trying to save that of five year old
Stephen.)*

Concorde clawing west grims
at the black eye of the Potomac

a Sea King rages at the pupil
like a bumblebee at a fisted blossom

blue men in pleasure boats
axe in a hush

a crocus yellows
naked as a rose out of its petals

on the spate of reportage
colouring tomorrow's press I see

the ice in the eye of the passer-by
the blue in the flotilla of yesterday

and my years that have passed
like the short span of Julie Moles

James Ballantyne

The Lloyd's Lament

Ah, listen to the Lloyd's lament;
A wealthy world in need.
All pennies paid, all rations spent
To meet the cost of greed.

For those who came to underwrite
In great alarm have found
Their ships capsizing overnight
and vessels run aground.

They never viewed the captain's log,
nor asked him if he knew
to navigate his way through fog
with such a careless crew.

And all because in better times,
when profits were the norm,
They hunted not for hidden crimes
to undermine the form.

And did those coffee - quaffing men
Three hundred years ago
Suspect their speculations then
would pioneer such woe?

Behold how Lloyd's is listing now
and see this ocean toss
Imperilled names who took the vow
of unrestricted loss.

And old school ties and alibis
Cannot prevent the root
of sugared cant and sweetened lies
from bearing bitter fruit.

Tess Pendle

Mates Letters Accuse MI6 of Nadir Plot

Nadir, Nadir, Nadir - a word meaning bottom or pit
Are we there or are we still sinking?
Corruption, debt, profit
Obsession with Under Our Noses,
Is leading us further away
From what's really important to nations who are
Destroying tomorrow today.

What's happened in Herzegovina
To the victims of Bosnia's shame,
Could happen to us while they're talking
Ensuring everyone else gets the blame.
It's the dirty, ragged shadow
With eyes too big for his head
Who'll tell you in a whisper
Why his father and mother are dead.

They were saying their prayers as usual
When some men came and took them away,
People talked through the night about Evil
Till the dawn of the murderous day
And they voted and voted and voted to agree
It was bad
That a boy from Gorasde
Had lost his mother and dad.

But, for the West, what's in the papers
About millionaires, MPs and crime
Takes our fancy more than the horrors
Of another place and time.
So be sure to remember that moment
When Nadir was the word we all used
We forgot the name of that orphan
So flim-flam kept us amused.
Be sure to remember that moment
When *we* not *they* stood accused.

Richard Anthony

Waste of Time

She was old and grey before her time
But her outward appearance was deceiving.
For inside lay the mind of a child
Piecing the fragments of memories together.

We were on the same wavelength. For I a child
Found great joy in her stories, but did not notice
Her face twist with pain trying desperately
To recall all that was lost.

She wept and stumbled upon her words
The train of thought so easily broken.
She found herself in a different world
A labyrinth with no way out.

Alzheimer's is that not what they call it,
A disease, stripping dignity and worth.
My grandmother, old and grey before her time
I believed she was becoming younger.

Donna Ellen Wilson

The Fortunes of War

The fortunes of war
have been Germany's fame
have been restored esteem and
eternal blame,
not
only freedom and peace
with no patriotism,
resurrection of cities
and flourishing wealth;
a
rent nation, rent people,
rent thoughts and rent feelings - men
fed up with being
ashamed of themselves.
Now frustration heats up in this
bursting boil, narrow minds
pouring hot oil
on an aching wound,
sowing
hypocrisy, hatred -
the fortunes of war
are a flaw
setting homes and emotions
in flames,

and clichés of
blond blue-eyed
blood-sucking killers
in sinister mirrors
arising again.

Gisa Braune

167

I Love a Poke in the Mouth

What's this?

Teeners from Holland and College Girls,
Tightly bound, showing their pearls.
Oil my cheeks, just ring for Dick,
Dial *s-e-x g-i-r-l-s*, stiffen your prick.

Some fool newsagent's slipped me a 'Sport'
With a 'special' on 'dirty dentists'
In which hard-up Karen's divulging her breasts -
Her lascivious lips reveal the rest -
Boasting, 'I love a poke in the mouth.'

Curvy-swingers, over-ripe humdingers,
Gorgeous glands, too heavy for hands,
Red-hot nipples and big-boob ripples,
Bazooms, inflated, to inflame grooms.

I recall Father took 'The News of the World'
For a touch of Sabbath frivolity,
And he'd be tiny-mind tickled with smutty small-ads
While everyone else ate their greens,
Oblivious to the 'pole' in his pants
Which threatened to upset our meals.

Bi-wives lead sordid lives
Rubber Mac has the knack
Making Randy a raver, Sally a shaver
While Wendy . . . wets her knickers.

Now the weight of 'The Times' maybe daunting,
But the message in tabloids is haunting and banal.

For dial-a-date, Master Bate,
Dial-date and masturbate,
Come at the tone, come at the groan,
But rest assured, you'll arrive alone.

S Kenny

Itch!

John Major's
Classless honours'
Clutch of starlit handful
Loses grip, to its pitfall:

Piles that hit the bottom:
Classless society's hard-gotten.

Paul Gerhard

My Lesbian Date by Sharon Stone

I have stones in my pockets
so I may drown
   as
the sea eats my ankles
I hear the cry of my sister
stoned under Islam
for taking a woman
to her naked breast
   my instinct tells me
that bisexual women
are afraid of the taste
   you tell me my kisses
are sweet
but there's the sour
hunger of women
who take marriage vows
to avoid
the stones
thrown

Maya Chowdhry

Headlines in Verse

is what
caught
my eye.

Not a thought
I presently link
with newsink.

These days the rhymes come wrong,
our lovely language stripped of song
and the senses starved of poetry.

Dear reader, this writer remains
constrained by predictability;
switch on the mains.

Stardrift and groundswell
voice space long
between the ears.

Andrew Wishart

Mrs Roosevelt Convoy Battle Was

a scrap of newsprint
from an out of date atlas
where a disappeared country
figured.
The war the fragment told of
erased the outline.

I placed it again in the atlas
in the page with the 'pronouncing index'
before the 'list of contractions'.
I here pronounce so many old names,
old countries,
so many wasted contractions
and pangs too.

Joan McGavin

173

Coming Out

A thousand
Lonely deaths
Had died
Before,
In their
Rehearsing;
But, tongued now,
Unexpectedly,
In a mouth
Dry as sandpaper,
The words,
When they came,
Fluttered into the
Space between them,
Light as air;
Planed slivers
Of his aching soul,
Wind-chiming
In the gentle breeze
Of a New Beginning,
Surprising him.

Bernie McClelland

Burning Conscience

Shop doorways
shelter the poor no more;
these homes
have become pyres
and mausoleums . . .
I heard the news:
this man - or woman
- no one knows -
was burned
beyond sex
not just recognition . . .
Are the destitute homeless
then
no-better than mere garbage
to be torched at vicious will?
Are we so flaming keen
to eradicate
embarrassing poverty?
Is this act of immolation
an indication
of transferred guilt
- deflected aggression?
Is there a desire
really
to scorch Third-World victims?
- which finding none
to burn
this side of the Telly
elects instead
to scorch our urban ones . . . ?
- Is this an act
of transference . . .
of burning conscience
in fact . . . ?!

Adrian Shaw

The Lawyers That Rape

Rape: a case of trial and terror. Not so for the men
In wigs who then compound man's error, raping once again.

Reality's perceived through what we see and hear and feel,
And when those senses are recalled, the scene once more is real.

So lawyers and police who seek to satisfy their thirst
For details are no better than the man who raped her first.

A victim, feeling used and dirty, fears the very thought
Of living through it all again, and seeing him in court.

And if she is a witness, she may seem quite unaffected,
But numbness is the price she pays to keep herself protected.

The girl who once was full of life is now an empty shell,
Who's scared of meeting anyone - alone inside her hell.

And so it is she's sentenced to a life of fear and pain.
The rapist though will soon walk free to go and rape again.

The man who rapes his daughter and expects his secret kept
Loves no one but himself and doesn't care how much she's wept.

As friend and as abuser he condemns her to a hell
Where future partners giving love will give abuse as well.

She's scared all day a friend may sense the shame she feels within,
And frightened when she goes to bed, in case her dad comes in.

So men - if you feel nothing when a rape is on the news,
Imagine what it might be like if you were in her shoes.

But if this brings back feelings that you wish would go away,
Then blame this verse for causing them and tear it out today.

Those feelings have protected you and got you where you are
And now you need some new resources, better ones by far.

So take a while to consider other ways to gain
The benefits those feelings grant but now without the pain.

And when you've finished, you may feel nothing's come to mind,
But burn this poem anyway and notice what you find.

Tony Pitcairn

When Matron Seduced a Schoolboy

When matron seduced a schoolboy
She should have approached him with caution
For the fidgeting she'd thought meant 'come hither'
Was merely the result of ant poison.

Bláithín Crombie

Classless Honours Much the Same

Classless honours much the same.
How reliably these lists appear
as petty deeds are rearranged.
A former banker made a Peer
an actress turned into a Dame,
to oil a stiffening social sphere
that bends the knee and gropes for fame.
Classless honours much the same.

We live in dull times now and all agree
that England is outpaced by world events.
Once we could not fail to honour victory
but have sunk to giving gongs for commonsense.
All we have left to conquer is our history
while the future holds no promise we can pay the rent.
This list is like a child's fort, which the sea
must shortly level to irrelevance.

Classless honours much the same.
The new crusade is to be fair
with pips and titles. Little's changed
except this seasonal search for gain
brings medals, sops and fancy names
to substitute for the welfare
of lord knows how much social pain.
Classless honours much the same.

Richard Baker

In Ermine Overall

In ermine overall
Serenely set in plushy seat in House of Lords,
Well britched against the economic chill,
The Labour Life Peer looks back on his life.
With no resentment for old comrades who,
In leisured hours
Outside the edifice of contrived idleness,
Dub him as pile of faeces and allege
An unknown factor in his parentage.
He still affirms retention of belief in
Emancipation of the working-class;
Though not so fast as once anticipated
But paced more modestly, one at a time.

Henry Jones

Tomahawks That go Astray

It happens to us all. That sudden red
says you have cut yourself somewhere
without realising it.

Irritation. It may blob the tablecloth,
blouse-cuff or silk tie. It stops you from
your business. Your body is disobeying orders.

Deduction at the sink. Its taps staunch
a scratch you cannot hear on a record.
Perhaps you determine how and why, perhaps not.

A dab of tissue, antiseptic if around,
and sticking plaster once found at the back
of a drawer where this slight injury goes

Forgotten inside five minutes. It never hurt,
there is no pain, it's one of those things,
there is no need to look closer - not again

At the darkening stain left to swell
newsprint from the banks of the Tigris,
Shibeli or the River Bosna

Before the body of war floods each back-ward
and corridor jammed with pain
Under a running tap of blood.

David Fine

United Nation States

A man that came to me
Said with frowned confusion,
'Are not states simply nations?'
I looked and nodded; agreed.

'Then is not the word united,
Of joined peoples and football teams,
The same in front of each?'
I stopped as shot; dumbfounded.

James R Canton

The Sound of Ayatollahs Finding Everlasting Peace

What was the sound
When his body dropped?

With cries and shouts and screams and shattered dreams
All around
Chatter, clatter, and wails of grief
To me it was a relief.

In Tianenmen Square
Students and poets
Doctors and peasants
Were gunned down by the brave 27th

At first it sounded like
Pop!
Gunfire never sounds like television.
Real guns 'pop'.
Car exhausts bang.

A gunshot pop
Sounds more like a car or a cracker
Just a gentle 'pop'
And the white shirt next to you
Falls down, dead.

But when the machine gun rattled
The poets and peasants knew it was true
The brave heroes of the 27th Army
Were shooting unarmed civilians
Men women and children
In the Streets of Everlasting Peace

But I want to know the sound when his body dropped
Was it a bang? a crash, a thump, a thud or a pop?
A million Khomeiniacs grabbed at his shroud
A sea of black, a swarming crowd
They loved him so much they tore him to shreds
Life everlasting's not worth much when your dead

No one heard that sound.
No one will ever know what it was like
In the crowd, screaming, believing, chanting, ululating,
One guy hit himself with an axe on the head
And an old limp corpse tumbled to the ground
Stone dead.

Did it thud or thump or was it eased down
What was the sound
Of falling Ayatollahs?

Was it a final *thud*?
Or a heavy resonant *thump*?
Did it go *pop* or *bonk* or *crunch*?
It's all too much for me
I think it went:
Rushdie.

David Langsam

Clinton Hails Strike a Success
Six Dead as Missiles Miss Iraqi Target

Shards of western morality
came searing
in moral indignation
through streets where prayer and hunger
go stalking hand in hand,

eclipsing the being of living souls:
six, or eight - or one hundred thousand -
the figures vary.
For it's quality, not quantity,
that counts.

Numbers are written in ciphers
from Africa to Guatemala
as souls are made to balance
the straightruled book
of market forces.

But the unspilled blood
of a president steeped in blood
cries out
in a voice a hundred million wails
cannot stifle.

Tom Bartlett

Clinton Acclaims Iraq Strike

Boy, we sure knocked those Iraqis flat
Said President Clinton to Socks the Cat

With laser-beamed intelligence and pinpoint accuracy
The most powerful man on Earth announced to the world
Don't tread on us Saddam!

Don't tread on us, and when shove comes to push
You shouldn't have messed with ex-President Bush

(Take it easy Bill, said Major, when given the word
And he was considerably supported by Douglas Hurd)

On the USS Chancellorsville near the Kuwaiti border
The admiral received his new world order
Tomahawks are go!

Twenty-three missiles rained in on Baghdad
Some went astray   and killed a few people
Which is undeniably sad
More bodies were   Layla al-Attar the celebrated
found in the rubble of   painter and her husband
Mansour suburb   buried under the ruins of their home

(Her Majesty's Opposition blustered and flustered
About dubious legality and suspect morality)

Ten thousand mourners in Baghdad demonstrated against
the cowardly terrorism falling from the skies

Hail to the Chief and salute America the winner

and somewhere in the Oval Office
Socks threw up his dinner

David Oliver

Wife's Plea

Dear John
Stop
I know
That we're married
Stop
And it's not
That I don't love you
Stop
But I don't want
To be raped by you
Anymore
Stop!

Terry Egan

Prison Hostage Drama Probe Call

Terror youth escape bid snatch
Hero warder freedom dash
Death threat knife ordeal
Safety review appeal.
Gaol conditions shock disclosure
Cell block drug abuse exposure:
Job cuts blame
Crisis claim
Group 4 row
Shake-up vow.

Newsflash headline word count squeeze
Reader story sense unease.
Writer hurry
Language worry:
Noun use rise
Syntax demise.

Alison Maddock

Six Hurt in Cockle War

Six men hurt in seaside scuffles,
A clash of giros on the shore.
Forget the winkles, whelks and mussels:
Remember the lost of a cockle war.

For here you will not find Kate Adie
Reporting from the battle zone;
Confirming what we know already:
Dogs will fight over any old bone.

The battle lines are clearly drawn -
It's 'us and them' in mutual fear.
The question breaking like the dawn:
Is nature owned by living near?

A clash of livelihoods, you see,
A sorry tale to spit and tell,
A symptom of a sickened country
Shrinking to a cockle shell.

Forced to pay for richer bungles,
The poor must pull themselves apart
And live in dog-eat dodgy jungles
That freeze the cockles of your heart.

Robert Mills

Agassi Dumped by Lover

There are some strange things in the news
to read and to discover,
yet something touching caught my eye
Agassi dumped by lover.

It seems he spends more time on court
than courting his young lady,
and finally she's had enough
and wants to go her own way.

So Agassi, sleek and tanned and fit
has had a nasty time of it,
misunderstood by love and life
and with no prospects of a wife
he boards his jet and travels home
as always, once again, alone.

Now, we are praised for being good
and we pay for being bad,
so I'm not surprised in Agassi's case
- have you seen *that* coffee ad?

Paul King

TV Lies of Mr Perfect

Echoes
Off the criss crossed banner.
The scheme of clenched teeth bulldogs,
All jut and sweat,
Who run
Between the littered exclamations
In the pages of The Sun.
Dirt dishers,
Pinched in suits,
Chasing their front page stories.
Those brought down,
Now tossed aside.
Each new shame
Heralding new glories.

Jeremy Noel-Tod

Springtime for Women Priests

Through meadows on the brink of rowdy summer
A road winds to a village that sits solid and unperturbed,
And on the road a figure as upright as her bike,
Prim and iron-backed - the Spinster;
Cycling through the dewy English morning,
Round the green, to communion.
Linger on that daffodil as she passes,
This timeless dream of England we chase
Even though we know it vanishes
At the first hot touch of hungry tongues.

But a bigger threat than our hunger glowers in the hedgerows,
The politician warns of mullahs, minarets;
'Pedal for your life England,' he urges, 'and I'll pedal dangerous
                                                         myths.'

Cut to wheels spitting gravel in flight; lose the pealing bells
To the melancholy wail of Islam,
See a city of shimmering domes and the intense sky
Where great updrafts of air buoy up spiralling birds and prayer.

But the Spinster - look again - here's a twist.
Hatless, ungloved, round and glossy with more,
A sermon crackling in her pocket under her cassock,
She nods at buds, half-built nests and other new beginnings,
But frowns:
'Women priests, *women* priests. It's women this and woman that.
'Shadow-men.
'Say priestess; cast our otherness in our own sun, not trailing in
                                                         yours;
'Say priestess; we are not strangers at altars.'

The politician staggers, bishops rise pale
At a pagan power awaking.
'Safeguards,' they hiss, 'safeguards have been agreed.
'*Woman* priest will do.'

Kym Martindale

Marital Rape

That bit you call my clit,
I call the heart
Of me; the part
I give to those who love,
Not shove.

The thing you call a ring,
A hole, leads to my soul.
Not to be entered lightly,
Nightly,
At your desire.

My fire burns
But only when I choose.
Too much to lose,
To hurt, to bruise -
And not just physically.
I have emotions, feelings,
I make love.

I won't be raped.
You tear me, wound me,
Scar my private part,
My inner secret self,
As if you cut my skin.
I bleed before your need
To fuck yourself on me.

Am I to you another screw?
No more?
A whore, a cunt, a bit of skirt?

Oh no, I'm me.
And if I choose to give myself
Then I come free.

Sue Wall

193

Crime and Passion in Bosnia

Sitting in a room of imperfect strangers
No thought of peace, impending dangers.
Bosnian, Serbian, Muslim, Slav
Taking what they want, defending what they have.

With foreign missiles, towns are razed
Power hungry warlords whose eyes are crazed
Expel the Muslims, destroy the mosques
Ethnic cleansing, whatever the costs

The UN send lorries, loaded with food
They wait at the border, forbidden to move
The people are starving, freezing and ill
What keeps them going? No more than their will.

Some towns are empty, buildings mere shells
Refugees need shelter, other towns swell
In peacetime five thousand, now multiplied by ten
But bread, water, meat, less than there were then.

They clamour for lorries, to escape from this mess
To get to a place where the suffering is less
Women and children are thrust to the fore
Some crushed, some suffocate, they'll suffer no more.

Damon Stephens

Fire Guts Historic Area of Lisbon

On the eve of your birth, unknown to us
Lisbon, old city, seethed and cried and burned.

As you flexed your limbs and freshly turned
To try your untried voice in an unknown land
Brick and plaster, worn by sea dew, scorched
And cafes cracked, the tea houses torched,
Pessoa - haunted rooms now ghosts themselves.
Strong and shouting, fresh and well, you seized
Breath, as smoke turned in an Atlantic breeze.

David Reddall

Half-Life on Earth

When we found the first Earth capsule
Trundling blindly round in space,
All that lay within convinced us
We should reach the human race.

The messages, once cracked, proved kind,
Art - odourless but bold.
The 'poems' seemed of little use
Though 'music' cured a cold.

And so we built a rocket ship
On a piece of level ground,
And all was set for lift-off till
Earth Capsule Two was found.

For this contained a deadly load,
That re-awoke old fears.
'It's plain they're at that nuclear stage -
Flight postponed a thousand years.'

John Hussey

Candle by the Bed

(at Hampton Court Palace)

First Voice   I heard today some faraway palace
                had caught on fire.
                Reporters talked of tapestries
                and priceless paintings
                plucked from gutted galleries.

                Some mention was made
                of a military widow
                too old to flee; but not,
                after all, as old as Art.
                (It was she, they said,
                who caused the fire to start.)

Second Voice   *All the old girl's neighbours said
                she'd kept a candle by the bed.*

First voice ˙   This brought to mind
                those likewise times
                when Wren rebuilt
                from blackened rubble.
                Now, once again,
                the treasures huddle modestly
                amid the ashes; singed,
                but still tinged with significance.

Second Voice   *All the old girl's neighbours said
                she'd kept a candle . . .*

197

First Voice   Fortunately for all concerned
(I also learned)
the best of the works
(by some quirk of fate)
were out at the cleaners
and escaped being burned.

Second Voice   *All the old girl's neighbours said*
   . . .

Leanne Weber

Wrappings - Double Food Bills

When we eat a piece of meat
Some cheese, a cake or bread
We've paid for more than food galore
In packaging, it's said.

So tell me why can't we fortify
With vitamins and taste
The bags and wraps around our snacks
And eat the lot - no waste!

J Casselden

Northern Heritage

Before the heat of summer
When bees hung honey-laden on the flower
And winds made velvet of the barley green,
I walked among the apple and sour cherry trees
Of Acorn Bank.
The only sound
Tornado Jets, Death's messengers
Above in Cumbrian skies.

Anthea Batty

Between Monsters

I met you by the river
And we walked,
We talked,
Oblivious to war
And death.
We were only passing through
From one side
To the other,
Together.
We had no differences
To fight about,
Only love
And hope,
And so we walked
And talked,
Together.
And, when he beckoned
From his ancient bed,
We too lay down,
Together,
And embraced.
And nights have come
And gone
And still we lie
Together,
Between monsters.

Mark Rogers